CITIZEN WARRIOR

Citizen Warrior

By Eugene W. Merritt Jr. and John H. Meyer

Cover, book design and layout
by John H. Meyer, Cape Fear Images

Illustrations are from the author's or co-author's collections, with these exceptions: Pages 71, 97, 100, 106, 110, 112, 116, 118, 124: North Carolina Manual (various editions), N.C. Secretary of State; Page 82: Shutterstock; Page 102: Exxon-Mobil; Page 109: U.S. Senate; Page 128: Rountree, Losee; Page 156: Amtrak

Printed in USA

ISBN: 978-0-9844900-7-3

Copyright 2025 Dram Tree Books

Publisher's Cataloging-in-Publication Data

Names: Merritt, Eugene Worth, 1944-, author. | Meyer, John H. 1953-, author.
Title: Citizen Warrior / by Eugene W. Merritt, Jr. and John H. Meyer.
Description: Wilmington, NC: Dram Tree Books, 2025.
Identifiers: ISBN: 9780984490073
Subjects: LCSH Merritt, Eugene Worth, 1944- .| Wilmington (N.C.)—Biography. | Wilmington (N.C.)—Planning. | Wilmington (N.C.)—History. | BISAC HISTORY / United States / State & Local / South (AL, AR, FL, GA, KY, LA, MS, NC, SC, TN, VA, WV) | BIOGRAPHY & AUTOBIOGRAPHY / Memoirs | ARCHITECTURE / Urban & Land Use Planning
Classification: LCC F264.W7 M35 2025 | DDC 975.627—dc23

Dram Tree Books
P.O. Box 7183
Wilmington, NC 28409
910-538-4076
www.dramtreebooks.com

CITIZEN WARRIOR

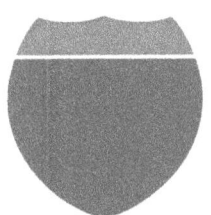

**Eugene W. Merritt, Jr.
and John H. Meyer**

Table of Contents

Paths to Success . . . . page 1
   Commitment to All the People in Your Community . . . . . . page 4

1. Reviving Downtown and DARE, Inc. . . . . page 7
   Downtown's Darkest Hours . . . . page 13
   A Deep-pocketed Ally and an Opening Agenda . . . . page 17
   Living Over the Store . . . . page 24
   Public Relations and Public Improvements . . . . page 28
   Creating Riverfest: A New Focus on the Cape Fear . . . . . page 33
   A Grant, a Park, and Lots of Public Investment . . . . page 40
   Evicting the 'Adult' Establishments . . . . page 45
   Spreading the Word, and Some Blunt Words . . . . page 48
   The Convention Center that Wasn't . . . . page 55
   A New Career and New Causes . . . . page 56

2. Liquor by the Drink . . . . page 63
   Organizing a Coalition . . . . page 65
   Reaching and Registering Young Voters . . . . page 68
   An Electoral Triumph Brings Economic Benefits . . . . page 73

3. Wilmington versus the Coal Pile . . . . page 79
   A Looming Threat to Downtown . . . . page 82
   Pro and Con Opinions and a Likely Done Deal . . . . page 86
   Finding a Loophole and Jumping through it . . . . page 90

4. Interstate 40 to Wilmington . . . . page 95
   You Can't Get There from Here . . . . page 99
   Finding the Federal Funding . . . . page 105
   Getting Our Slice from a Shrinking State Pie . . . . page 111
   Playing Games in the Legislature . . . . page 114
   'Some Little Road to New Hanover County' . . . . page 117
   A New Governor Keeps his Promise . . . . page 123

Table of Contents

5. Other Windmills to Tilt at ....page 133
    Creating the River-to-the-Sea Rotary Run............page 133
    Extending Revitalization up North Fourth Street ......page 134
    Water Street Center ....page 142
    Saving 'One Tree Hill' ....page 145
    Governor's Landing.................................page 150
    Saving our Hospital ....page 152
    Reviving Passenger Rail Service....................page 155
    Landmark Status for New Hanover High School ......page 158

6. What Makes a Citizen Warrior ....page 163

Appendix
    About the Author..................................page 169
    Gene Merritt's Organizations and Affiliations ....page 171
    About the Co-author ....page 171

Index ....page 175

Paths to Success

Imagine an alternative Wilmington, North Carolina. Not the vibrant, growing community we live in now: A magnet for vacationers, retirees, artists, and entrepreneurs. Not the place where people by the thousands want to live, want to visit, want to open new businesses. Our hypothetical Wilmington is a place where most young people leave town to find good jobs as soon as they graduate from high school or college, just as so many had to do in the 1960s, 1970s, and 1980s.

That was true for me. Wilmington offered me no opportunities to pursue my ideal profession, marketing and public relations. I tried teaching. I worked for a time in my family's business. I tried publishing, with "niche" magazines focused on the arts and on real estate. But to really take advantage of my education, and do the work I was best suited for, I had to move away. For three years in the early 1970s, I was executive director of the United Arts Council, Inc. of Greensboro.

In 1975, wanting to return to Wilmington, I decided to take a chance and re-start the public relations and communications business I'd run a few years earlier. As these stories will show, that move proved invaluable, especially in making political connections that eventually would have a big payoff. But opportunities here were still sharply limited; our community's future still looked very hazy.

* * *

Instead of what it's like today, visualize Wilmington as it very well might have shaped up over the past half century. How this city would look if certain important battles had never been fought. Or if those battles' outcomes had been different.

- Instead of the bustling dining, nightlife and performing-arts scene we see downtown, where the streets are thronged with locals and tourists both day and night, picture decaying buildings with boarded-up store windows, their upper stories derelict and empty. Visualize a business district dominated by pornography shops, strip clubs, and skid-row bars: Dirty, dangerous, and deserted.
- Instead of the Wilmington Convention Center, hotels, multiple concert venues, marinas and restaurants, and hundreds of residential condos on downtown's north end, imagine a huge mountain of coal, rumbling freight trains, and acres of crumbling, abandoned industrial buildings.
- Instead of an easy two-hour drive up Interstate 40 to Raleigh, imagine that the only connections between our little city and our state capital consist of a tangle of two-lane roads, none of them even a direct route. Imagine slow-moving farm machinery and dozens of small-town stoplights making travel an endless, inconvenient ordeal. In place of the thriving new hotels, busy retail centers, and upscale neighborhoods, bolstered by the new residents, new industry, and new vacationers that the interstate brought to town, visualize a stagnant, depressed business community, struggling to hang on.
- Instead of the many excellent restaurants downtown, at the beaches, and in fact all over town, think of a handful of eateries struggling to make a profit, forbidden to sell a customer a cocktail with dinner. Think of restaurants limited by law to letting patrons pour their own drinks from a personal liquor bottle hidden inside a brown-paper bag. Think of out-of-town visitors bemused and disappointed that they aren't allowed to buy such a basic amenity as a mixed drink, routine in other vacation destinations.
- Instead of the many elegant dining spots all along the Cape Fear River waterfront or on the Intracoastal Waterway, visualize empty wharves and piers on which it's illegal to serve food or drink.

That's how Wilmington might have ended up today, had it not been for an aggressive downtown-revitalization effort. Had it not been for a years-long advocacy campaign to get an Interstate Highway built. Had a massive coal-exporting terminal been allowed to blight the city's northern waterfront. Had our county's voters not been persuaded to approve the sale of liquor by the drink. Had legislators not been pressured and persuaded to overturn an arbitrary and unnecessary environmental regulation.

Newcomers to town may take these accomplishments for granted, but they were hard-won. They were earned in the face of stiff opposition from powerful forces that wanted to lock us into a status quo that benefitted only a fortunate few.

So how were those victories won? To be sure, accomplishing those goals required big coalitions. They included elected officials and government bureaucrats, business owners and bankers, lobbyists and legislators, news media and civic groups, and ordinary citizens: Voters. But before any of those necessary coalitions took shape, it was engaged, activist citizens, pushing and prodding and refusing to take "No" for an answer, who got the ball rolling. Who jump-started grass-roots movements for change. Who recruited allies and nudged public opinion and found creative ways to get around "the way it had always been done."

I call these kinds of people "Citizen Warriors." And based on my own experience in helping to accomplish these transformative changes to my home town, I hope to inspire others to play similar roles, to achieve today's important civic goals. These stories of successful Citizen Warrior battles in recent decades may offer insight into how to win other important battles in the future.

* * *

I hope you find these stories interesting and that they encourage you to become more involved in helping your community by being a Warrior. By that term, I mean a person who is willing to fight for what is right and good for all the people.

The final chapter deals with various attributes critical to becoming a community leader. I don't expect anyone to be totally effective in every category, but the more of the attributes you can achieve, the better.

The concept of this book is to present those attributes of community leadership along with real-life examples of people who exhibit those qualities. Although much of what follows concerns my various adventures, this book is equally about the innumerable allies and collaborators who helped to accomplish so many important objectives.

Just to make the record clear about how and why I got involved in all these causes, let me give you some information about my background.

I was born the son of a son of a poor tobacco farmer from the Magnolia, North Carolina area. His family was so poor that his parents could not afford to send my father to college. Yet, my father was one of the most intelligent persons I have ever met.

Eugene Worth Merritt (my father) was my co-Citizen Warrior. He was by my side in my efforts to improve my community and state. I will never forget his efforts and I will always be indebted to him.

I was not born rich nor entitled in any manner. I had no political power in the beginning, though that would change over the years.

My own early career was like many others who grew up in Wilmington; our home town offered very limited economic opportunities. My 1966 degree in English from UNC-Chapel Hill prepared and encouraged me to gravitate toward a career in marketing and communication, specifically advertising and public relations. But Wilmington in those days offered few such opportunities. After trying various ventures that didn't pay well, I left town for a while.

But when I returned to Wilmington in 1975, I decided to take a chance and start a firm of my own again. One of my specialties was managing political campaigns. I helped several candidates get elected to important positions, which would prove to be very important in the next few years. But opportunities here were still sharply limited; our community's future still looked very hazy. What it would take to change that is what this book is about.

Along with the stories of other Citizen Warriors, I will cover some of the great adventures that my father and I, with significant help from my brother, embarked on.

Commitment to All the People in Your Community

Commitment is the foundation of the process of becoming a community leader. To be an effective Citizen Warrior, it is critical that you possess this trait. Rest assured, leaders will be tested. They will be confronted. By supporting your causes, you will make enemies. There are those who will resent your actions, often because you could cause cost them money or power. Sometimes your opponents will say and do things that are extreme and excessive, and sometimes dangerous.

To make progress against such headwinds, you must love your community and all the people who live there. You must have a firm and unwavering commitment to promoting the health and welfare of your community—*all* the people. Failure to uphold this principle will lead to dissension from disparate groups. If everyone knows that you support the entire community, without regard to politics or religion, you will stand a much better chance of winning their support when needed.

You can be a Democrat or a Republican or Independent, but you cannot allow the political philosophies associated with those groups to compromise your words or actions when it comes to promoting the public good.

Regardless of what you, as a community leader, are working on, there will always be naysayers and disrupters. You must maintain the strength to push though these potential obstacles. You must remember you are working to achieve what is in the best interests of all the people.

I have to make particular mention of the news media. In many of the battles this book describes, a combination of thorough if sometimes skeptical news reporting and consistent editorial-page support was invaluable in helping the general public understand what we were trying to do, and why it was important. Without ignoring TV news departments, which also played important roles in these stories, let me say I regret the decline of daily print journalism. Changes in technology and mass-media economics have badly hurt local newspapers everywhere, including here in Wilmington.

During the twentieth-century heyday of what's now called the *StarNews* (it was the *Morning Star* and *Sunday Star-News* during my work downtown, the fight to build I-40, and most of the other stories I'll tell here) I got plenty of news coverage as well as strong editorial backing. That depended both on healthy relationships with reporters and on cultivating media leaders: Publishers and top editors. From the 1970s onward, the newspaper has been supportive of everything I've ever done in the public realm. Fortunately, in its most influential years, the *Star-News* was able to make a significant difference in public understanding of critical issues—and in rallying public support.

Of course, you can never please all the people all the time, but that cannot stop you from achieving your goals.

The author in the mid-1970s as he was beginning his work with DARE, Inc. and downtown revitalization.

During my time working to revitalize downtown Wilmington, I made some dangerous enemies. In the late 1970s, downtown was plagued by a cluster of disreputable businesses: Topless bars and adult bookstores, not to mention the prostitutes roaming the streets. My tactics to mitigate this blight included buying buildings that housed some of these establishments and evicting them, and enacting restrictive zoning that would force the rest out of downtown.

During this process, I was approached by the owner of one of those adult-entertainment businesses. He warned me to stop what we were doing—or risk loss of life.

In other words, he threatened to kill me. I found out later that a number of those businesses were owned and operated by organized crime groups. Despite the threats, we did not back down. We hung in there and persevered. I never told my wife and family about these threats because I knew they would worry.

I think this is a good example of an unwavering commitment to the welfare of our community and an example of creativity in our leadership efforts. I hope it is an encouragement to other Citizen Warriors, wherever they are located.

1. Reviving Downtown and DARE, Inc.

Downtown Wilmington in the mid-1970s was like all too many of America's central business districts. It had seemingly been made obsolete by the suburbs and by the growth of highways and the decline of mass transit. Like other struggling downtowns, it had become a drain on public budgets and a haven for crime.

Here, the exodus of retailers from downtown had begun in the 1950s, when Wilmington's first suburban shopping centers were built. One of them, Hanover Center, had lured the Sears, Roebuck & Co. department store away in the '60s. After Sears left, downtown began to deteriorate. Other small retailers joined Sears' departure, leaving more and more buildings empty. Building owners, if they could find tenants at all, started renting to disreputable businesses.

As in so many cities, "urban renewal" was tried as a solution. And as in so many other places, it created its own set of problems. In Wilmington, the city's "Redevelopment Commission" tore down much of the old Atlantic Coast Line Railroad's infrastructure, including the train station and office buildings. The agency also demolished two blocks' worth of Nineteenth-Century warehouse buildings along north Water Street. In their place, in 1966, it built a large parking deck at a cost of $750,000. That was equivalent to $7.4 million in 2025 dollars.

Later, the Redevelopment Commission would try a couple of other gimmicks in hopes of stimulating downtown business. In 1971 and 1972, it

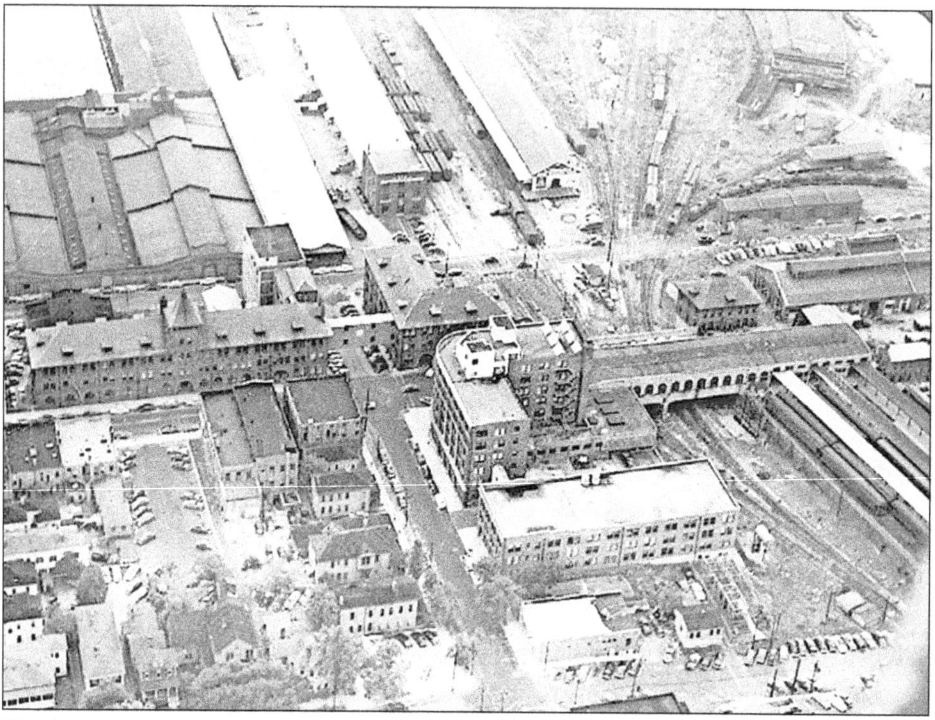

The Atlantic Coast Line Railroad dominated Wilmington in the 1950s. North Front Street now runs where the passenger concourse once straddled the tracks. The Cape Fear Community College now occupies much of the former ACL property. The two warehouses at the top remain as the Coast Line Conference Center. The Wilmington Convention Center now stands where railroad tracks ran in the picture's upper right corner.

Union Station, in this century-old postcard image, stood at the corner of North Front and Red Cross Streets. Built by the Atlantic Coast Line railroad, it was the center of the ACL's headquarters complex, which occupied downtown's north end.

In 1970, a decade after the ACL moved its headquarters to Jacksonville, Florida, Union Station was demolished. Next door, one building survived and served as Wilmington's Police Station, but has since been torn down. Only two former railroad buildings remain.

spent $320,000 on a walkway that connected the parking deck to the rear doors of many stores on North Front Street. Finally, in 1974, it rebuilt North Front Street, with a single one-way traffic lane and angle parking, and a pedestrian-only block next to what's now The Cotton Exchange. That work, costing more than $400,000, did little or nothing for downtown, proved unpopular with both merchants and the public, and eventually would be eliminated entirely.

But at least somebody was trying something.

* * *

Among those trying to fight back against neglect and decay were two visionary partners. In the cluster of historic buildings that had once housed the Sears store, Joseph Reaves and Malcolm Murray were taking a huge risk. After their property was damaged by a fire, they first considered tearing everything down. Then they got a better idea: Create a prototype for a new kind of urban shopping center. When The Cotton Exchange opened in 1976, it was among the nation's pioneers in repurposing old buildings as nostalgic clusters of boutiques, eateries, and offices.

I think it's fair to say that Joe Reaves and Mal Murray saved downtown Wilmington from the wrecking ball by their example in sparing The Cotton Exchange. When DARE, Inc. got started, one of our early priorities was to return the favor by opening Front Street again, just as The Cotton Exchange was proving its value as an "anchor" for retailing downtown. Of course, we also believed reopening the street would encourage better traffic circulation throughout downtown.

By 1975, the year before the Cotton Exchange opened, a new threat to downtown was visible on the horizon. A major Wilmington developer, Hugh MacRae II, in partnership with out-of-town interests, had announced plans to build the city's first indoor shopping mall. The proposed Independence Mall threatened to drive the last nails into the coffin of downtown's retail community.

The two remaining downtown department stores, J.C. Penney and Belk-Beery, were almost certain to join Sears as anchors for that new regional mall. The few smaller stores still open were likely to follow, as many of them ultimately did. Already, the flight of retailers to the suburbs had left downtown's shopping streets a shadow of their former selves. Storefront after storefront sat empty. The display windows of one vacant building (now an exclusive, high-end restaurant) were stacked with bales of peat moss, serving as a cheap warehouse for a nearby garden-supply store. Most of that property's neighbors either were vacant or had their windows painted over. Behind those sleazy façades operated so-called "adult" bookstores, which in those pre-video days sold mostly pornographic magazines; and so-called "topless" bars. Like the topless joints, another cluster of bars on South Front Street, which their own patrons called "skid row," catered to a rough crowd, such as bikers or Marines from Camp Lejeune. Already, downtown had a reputation as a place to be avoided, especially after dark.

With few exceptions, such business as remained in the officially designated Central Business District took place at street level. The upper floors of most of downtown's Nineteenth- and early-Twentieth-Century buildings were dark and dusty, their former tenants having long since fled to newer office space elsewhere.

The buildings that would become The Cotton Exchange as they looked in 1973. The retail and dining complex would open in 1976.

Another widespread problem: During the 1950s and early '60s, in misguided attempts at "modernization," too many elegant older buildings had been mutilated. Decorative architectural details had been hacked off and ugly false fronts made of metal or concrete attached to hide the buildings' original appearance.

That was the situation in 1975. I had just returned to Wilmington after my three-year tenure with the United Arts Council, Inc. of Greensboro. Back home again, I started my own public relations and communications business. That career was natural enough; my 1966 degree in English from UNC-Chapel Hill had prepared and encouraged me to gravitate toward marketing, advertising, and public relations. During this period, I founded several publications and started managing political campaigns. I was successful in helping several candidates get elected to public office.

One of those was Ben Halterman. I agreed to run his 1975 campaign for mayor. Halterman was an insurance agent who had been elected to the City Council in 1971. With his four-year term as councilman about to expire, he decided to try for a two-year term as mayor, taking advantage of a recent amendment to the City Charter. That now allowed voters to directly elect our mayor, who was also a voting member of the Council. This was

In 1978, Market Street (like nearby Front Street) was lined with topless bars and 'adult' bookstores. Evicting those businesses was a vital accomplishment in DARE's early years.

a change from the old system, by which the Council had picked the mayor from among its own members.

He was running against an entrenched incumbent, the retired General Herbert Brand, who had first become mayor under the old charter: Elected by his Council peers, not by the city's voters. My challenge: Present Ben Halterman as a voice for Wilmington's future, not its past.

Downtown was an obvious issue for me. With the planned mall threatening to put an end to mass merchandising downtown, I believed some affirmative action needed to be taken. As a loyal and dedicated Wilmingtonian who cared deeply about the future of both downtown and the city as a whole, I urged Halterman to make revitalizing downtown a major campaign issue.

It worked. We won the 1975 election in an upset. Ben and I became truly bonded at that point, sharing in the glory. In office, he followed through, taking the lead in establishing a new urban redevelopment organization.

I helped Mayor Halterman develop the model for a non-profit, tax-exempt corporation that would be jointly funded by the City of Wilmington, New Hanover County, and the private sector. I also helped him get approval and funding from both the City Council and the New Hanover County Commissioners for that new entity.

As mayor in the late 1970s, the late Ben Halterman kicked off Wilmington's downtown revitalization efforts.

The first step was establishing the Mayor's Task Force for City Core Revitalization, which included both government and business people. Notably, those members included two visionary developers: Joe Reaves of The Cotton Exchange, and Thomas Wright, Jr., a member of an important Old Wilmington family. (In addition to owning the Wright Chemical Co. in nearby Acme, N.C., he was one of the Wrights of Wrightsville Beach.) Later he would develop Chandler's Wharf, which became a vital southern anchor for downtown. Just as important, he would provide crucial behind-the-scenes financial help over the next few years.

But I'm getting ahead of myself. In October 1976, the Mayor's Task Force presented its report to the City Council. It endorsed a strategy of recruiting business, restoring historic buildings, and finding new sources of money. The Task Force also agreed with my recommendation that a public-private partnership would be the best long-term structure to carry out those objectives.

The presentation to the Council included a slide show "dealing with physical aspects of the downtown problem," as a contemporary summary put it. This included answers to the question "Why revitalization now?" Those included the fact that valuable commercial buildings, if left idle, will deteriorate, catch fire, "or fall into misuse," housing pornography shops or disreputable bars. "The physical environment of the downtown continues to deteriorate with the passage of time," the report warned.

The report also urged a focus on the Cape Fear River "as a major people-oriented resource." Tom Wright would be a pioneer in that effort.

The Task Force concluded that downtown's problems were complex enough that a new organization with a full-time staff would be needed, to be "the vital catalyst which turns ideas into realities." Thus we proposed that the city create what was referred to by the generic "Downtown Development Organization," to have a $57,000 annual budget, two-and-a-half-person staff, and a large governing board.

The City Council agreed, unanimously.

Downtown's Darkest Hours

Preparing to incorporate this new entity, we realized it needed a better name. And so with the city government's help, we held a public contest. The winning submission was the acronym DARE, for "Downtown Area Revitalization Effort." In May, 1977, we incorporated under that name.

I was one of five incorporators. In addition to representatives from the City Council, the Board of County Commissioners, and the downtown merchants' association, the fifth incorporator would prove a vital ally. That was Frederick Willetts III, better known as Rick, whose family owned and managed the Cooperative Savings & Loan Association. He had chaired the Mayor's Task Force. He and I were among the twenty-nine members of DARE's first Board of Directors. Rick Willetts would become that board's first president.

That large Board of Directors was meant to ensure that every group with a stake in downtown's success had a seat at the table. Slots were reserved for city and county officials, representatives from relevant state agencies, the downtown merchants' association, bankers, and residents of the adjacent Historic District.

Among our first tasks was to lobby for public financial support, based on the concept of a third each from the city, the county, and the private sector. DARE was chartered as a non-profit, tax-exempt entity that could legally receive public and donated money. That meant private contributions would be tax-deductible. We could now officially lobby the local governments and solicit private contributions, and we succeeded in getting budget support to start operations.

In August 1977, the City Council released the $10,000 it had pledged to get DARE started. That was an important incentive to get the County Commissioners to do the same. Private donors kicked in another $12,000. So by January 1978, we were fully in business.

Already, the brand-new DARE board had used money from a federal job-creation grant to hire our first employee, a young real-estate appraisal expert. His initial job description was "promotion coordinator." It would take us several more months to find and hire our top administrator, DARE's first executive director.

But even while searching for the right person for that job, we were developing ideas. Most ambitious (and, sadly, ahead of its time) was a proposed marketing plan. We hoped to get merchants to contribute funds for a joint newspaper advertising campaign to promote downtown as a shopping destination. That idea would remain a dream for many years; trying to get promotional money from dozens of merchants was like herding cats. Year after year, merchants' reluctance to invest in a joint marketing campaign would frustrate our attempts toward that goal.

We were more successful with some other early objectives. Those included building a shaky alliance with a new city manager; developing design guidelines for downtown buildings to defend against any more misguided "modernizations"; and finding a way to compel property owners to do a minimum level of maintenance on their buildings. Then there was the matter of traffic circulation.

Even as early as January 1978, members of DARE's Executive Committee were talking about the North Front Street pedestrian mall as a problem, which aggravated "an already unsatisfactory circulation situation," according to that month's meeting minutes. As for that closed-off block next to The Cotton Exchange, the Executive Committee noted, "improvements promised by the city were never delivered and that section remains unfinished."

With The Cotton Exchange as an impressive early example of what revitalization could mean for downtown, it was no accident that when we finally hired our executive director, he would be a retailer who owned a small chain of shops, one of them in that very development. His hiring certainly reassured the retailers on that first Board of Directors that they would have a useful ally. But maybe we should have paid more attention to what he said when first applying for the job. "Because of changes in my business, I am consolidating my businesses in Wilmington," he wrote to the DARE board's hiring committee.

We were also impressed by our new hire's credentials as an advertising expert; he had worked for some of the nation's leading ad agencies. That fact led to one important staff change, as the board minutes explain: "Since DARE's executive director is one of the top advertising promotion men in the country, Mr. Willetts proposed . . . that the title of promotion coordinator

Ornamental pavement seen here on Front Street at The Cotton Exchange was a remnant of a well-intended 1973 'pedestrian mall' that interfered with downtown's traffic circulation.

be changed to that of assistant director." We voted to approve that, and were happy to be off and running.

Two weeks into his new job, the new director presented several agenda items at the April 1978 Board meeting. Those included replacing damaged or diseased trees along downtown's streets, and encouraging the New Hanover County Commissioners to choose a downtown site for a proposed new public library. So far, so good!

And then things blew up in our faces.

Our executive director, as it turned out, had serious financial problems of his own. His business was on the verge of bankruptcy. When he'd mentioned "consolidating" his business, it meant he'd been forced to close his stores in Jacksonville and Fayetteville, and the Wilmington location wouldn't be far behind. He'd been on the job barely thirty days before we discovered this and some other questionable issues with his background. We decided to fire him.

At the time, DARE's public position was that our board had "accepted his resignation," which was characterized as being "for personal reasons." But whether he'd actually quit or been fired was beside the point. He was gone.

And then here we were, an exciting, brand-new, up-and-coming organization—with no top management. Once again, we had to rely on our assistant director to keep the doors open. And we, as a board, had to come up with a better candidate for the top job. But who?

* * *

Rick Willetts, DARE's first president, encouraged the author to become the organization's director.

It wasn't long after this when my phone rang. It was Rick Willetts. He invited me to join him and some other folks for dinner. Over a good meal and some good Jack Daniel's—poured from a bottle hidden in a brown paper bag in those days before liquor by the drink was legal—Rick and the others talked me into taking the executive director's job.

For the record: I'd had no plans to lobby for this. The previous year, when the search for an executive director first began, I'd been gainfully employed at the State Ports Authority. And even after I lost that job in September 1977 (as described in a later chapter) I was fortunate to bounce back with another state job. But soon enough I decided to consider other options. While contemplating re-opening my public relations firm, I had tested the employment waters by briefly throwing my hat into the ring for DARE's top job. Nothing came of that.

After that position got filled and then became vacant again, I didn't consider myself to be in the job market anymore. My firm was doing well. Now that DARE was up and running, my seat on its board was plenty for me. But Rick was very persuasive. I know now that Rick himself had been strongly encouraged to become DARE's first president. His father, a public-spirited executive who ran Cooperative S&L, had urged him to take that

The 'Morning Star' reported on the author's hiring as DARE's second executive director after his predecessor's very brief time in the job.

high-profile but risky position, before any of us could be certain our efforts would succeed.

But despite inevitable ups and downs, triumphs and disappointments, we did succeed.

DARE, Inc. became the first public-private partnership of its type in the history of North Carolina. The primary motivation of both city and county governments was financial: Encouraging the growth of tax base and jobs and making downtown attractive to tourists. Those goals turned out to be prophetic.

When Rick Willetts introduced me as executive director at the June 1978 Board meeting, it was the beginning of a four-year commitment. I would hold that job until the middle of 1982. According to the minutes, "Mr. Merritt remarked that he was pleased to have been appointed to the position and would work hard to fulfill the policies and goals of the organization."

Those minutes included several other major accomplishments. We learned that the city manager had put $30,000 in his budget to re-open that awkward "pedestrian mall" to traffic. We also learned that the County Commissioners had agreed that the much-needed new library would be downtown. (Eventually, the county would acquire and remodel the building the Belk-Beery department store vacated when it moved to Independence Mall.) We discussed the economic benefits that would come when the U.S. Coast Guard icebreaker *Northwind*, with its crew of 150 and $2 million payroll, found a new home port in Wilmington. (That was largely thanks to our congressman, U.S. Rep. Charles G. Rose III. It wouldn't be the last time Charlie Rose proved to be a vital ally for Wilmington and our surrounding communities, notably in the long fight to get an Interstate Highway built. But that's a story for another chapter.)

A Deep-Pocketed Ally and an Opening Agenda

Another very welcome development in 1978 was the opening of a hugely important new commercial complex, Chandler's Wharf.

The year before, one of DARE's founding board members, Thomas Wright, Jr., had bought the riverfront property at the foot of the bluff between Ann and Nun Streets. For the next year, he worked to transform the site into a re-creation of what Wilmington's working urban waterfront had looked like in its heyday.

He bought historic buildings elsewhere and moved them to the site; they would house shops, a restaurant, and a maritime museum. To further the museum's mission, he bought half a dozen historic boats. Some of them, such as an old wooden-hulled steam tugboat, were mounted on shore as static displays. Two remained in the water as attractions: The *Captain J.N. Maffitt*, a former Navy launch that soon would be carrying sight-seers on river tours, and the *Harry W. Adams*, a Nova Scotia "Bluenose" schooner of the sort that used to ply the coastal trade.

"We needed some sailing ships in the Historic District, with masts in the air and flags flying," Wright was quoted in a *Morning Star* feature on his project.

Wright repaved a stretch of Water Street with stone "Belgian blocks"—originally brought here as ballast in sailing ships—as it would have looked a century earlier. Left intact among the paving stones was a remnant of the railroad tracks that had once served all of downtown's wharves.

When Chandler's Wharf opened in 1978, its most revolutionary element was the brand-new Pilot House restaurant. At the time, nobody could predict whether dining with a river view would appeal to customers. So the menu started out modest, just sandwiches and salads. Diners would place their orders at a window, collect their food on paper plates, and sit down to eat on open-air tables sheltered only by umbrellas.

And to everybody's surprise, perhaps even including Tom Wright's, it was a huge success. Soon the Pilot House would recognize the untapped potential of its location, and began the first in a years-long series of additions that would enclose the original deck, add a new one, and upgrade the menu. What had begun as a casual sandwich shop quickly evolved into the seafood-forward fine-dining establishment that it's been ever since.

Meanwhile, the maritime museum wasn't paying for itself, even with the considerable draw of an authentic wooden schooner open for tours. Eventually, Wright closed the museum, although many of its exhibits remained in place. In 1984, after the next-door Pilot House had proved how profitable waterside dining could be, the former museum became a second restaurant, Elijah's.

Well before then, high demand for the complex's few retail spaces had justified an expansion into a rehabilitated building across Ann Street. (That expansion would become part of a sprawling federal grant-supported project, which I'll get to shortly.) And besides serving as a solid southern anchor

The Pilot House restaurant in Chandler's Wharf proved riverfront dining was a winning business strategy. Its success encouraged other restaurants to open along the Cape Fear River, and led its owners to expand and upgrade what had begun as a sandwich shop.

for the revitalized downtown, Chandler's Wharf had proved that waterfront dining was both appealing to customers and profitable for restaurants.

I'll return later to the matter of riverside restaurants.

This story wouldn't be complete without mentioning how much help Tom Wright would give to DARE over the years, helping us to finance some essential real estate purchases. As I'll explain, he deserves thanks for our successful campaign to boot the sleazy sex-oriented businesses out of downtown, as well as for DARE's purchase of the old railroad warehouses that would become the Coast Line Center.

* * *

Getting back to my first DARE meeting as executive director: We heard that the City of Wilmington would be applying for a major federal "urban development" grant. By leveraging millions in private money, including Tom Wright's extension of Chandler's Wharf, that grant would encourage dozens of new business investments. Most visibly, that money eventually would transform our waterfront, creating downtown's first riverside park and the beginnings of today's miles-long Riverwalk.

Those were all highly encouraging developments, certainly a great start to my new job. Remember, it would still be another year before the largest-ever exodus of retailers from downtown. So we had to seize on every possible advantage as we prepared for the looming opening of Independence Mall.

For those who weren't around then, it may be useful to compare some figures from 1978 with the situation in downtown Wilmington today.

- The value of all private property in the Central Business District was $36 million (about $175 million in today's dollars, if adjusted for inflation). In 2025, property in that same area, including dozens of major new buildings, was valued at more than $760 million.
- The number of people working downtown was estimated at 5,000. That's still not an easy statistic to get, but the present-day numbers are undoubtedly several times that.
- Cape Fear Technical Institute had 2,000 students. Now called Cape Fear Community College, its student body numbers over 15,000—although some of those attend classes at newer outlying campuses.
- City and county taxes, both property and sales, from downtown amounted to $1 million in 1978. For 2024, property tax collections alone totaled over $9.6 million. Sales tax numbers are harder to come by, but undoubtedly have grown, too. Downtown today has far more retail establishments, including many, many restaurants, than it did in 1978.

That year, before so many of them moved to the mall, downtown had more than eighty retail stores, including two major department stores, two pharmacies, several big discount places—what we used to call dime stores—and a long list of jewelers and clothing stores.

As of early 2025, according to Wilmington Downtown, Inc. data, the number of retailers downtown is close to ninety. But as we predicted in the 1970s, those are mostly specialty businesses.

* * *

By the time I got settled into my new job, I had drafted a road map for the coming year. It was called "Synopsis of DARE Work Program." I presented it at my second Board meeting as executive director, in July 1978. Objectives I intended to pursue were:

- Draft design guidelines for downtown's commercial buildings, plus a city ordinance that would impose minimum standards for their maintenance.

- Arrange financing, mostly through federal Small Business Administration loans, for merchants wanting to open up shop or expand.
- Establish a revolving loan fund, to help building owners remove ugly façades. That first year, the fund held $25,000, but we needed more. We had already asked the city to bolster the loan pool with another $50,000 from the following year's federal Community Development Block Grant.
- Develop a centralized management system for downtown retailers, to operate much as shopping centers do, with the minimum goal of coordinating marketing, promotions, and streetscape improvements.

That "Work Program" document also listed the challenges we were facing:

- Recruiting new businesses, even as existing stores were being lured away.
- Improving downtown's traffic flow and the availability of parking.
- Upgrading downtown's esthetics. This involved not just stripping off the ugly false fronts from many buildings, but also evicting the sleazy "adult" businesses, and encouraging improvements to public streets and sidewalks.
- Ensuring that the city and county governments would keep their financial commitments.

Fortunately, both city and county remained helpful partners. For example, at the August 1978 board meeting, I was able to announce that the Wilmington Transit Authority (predecessor to today's Wave Transit) was about to start a free mini-bus shuttle service to help visitors get around downtown. It linked Chandler's Wharf, the Cotton Exchange, and downtown's historic attractions like Thalian Hall and the Burgwyn-Wright House. Today's free downtown "trolley" bus route, operated by Wave Transit, is a direct descendant of that first shuttle.

During the next several months, we took other important steps.

In October 1978, we hired an advertising agency, which for the time being would continue to concentrate on print media.

We announced that our loan fund had lent $17,000 so far, to help with renovation or purchase of four buildings.

In November, the Executive Committee gave DARE's endorsement to a pending referendum to permit restaurants to sell liquor by the drink.

That would be a major change in state and local alcohol rules. I had gotten deeply involved in that cause, which was backed by downtown's then-small restaurant community. I tell the full story of that effort in the next chapter.

* * *

One seemingly trivial event in 1978 spoke volumes about downtown's potential as a place for music and entertainment. At that time, a skilled woodworker named Jim Nicholson had set up shop in a vacant retail building in the first block of South Front Street. His business, Design Workshop, was creating reproduction door and window frames, ornamental brackets, and other fancy architectural details. He sold these first to residents restoring old houses in the nearby Historic District and then to developers tackling similar projects in the Central Business District. But on Halloween night, 1978, Nicholson hosted a party. He pushed his workbenches together to form a stage for a band; and a diverse crowd of downtown merchants, developers, and enthusiasts—including quite a few DARE board members—turned up in costume to eat, drink, dance, and have a great time. That event predicted what downtown would eventually become: A fun, attractive place for the arts, amusements, and socializing by people of all kinds.

In November, DARE's board agreed to begin paying my dues to the Wilmington Rotary Club, which I had joined the year before. My dues were covered, as the minutes stated, "because his membership was based on his employment as Executive Director of DARE, Inc." That wasn't unusual. Many enterprises, then and now, encourage their executives to get involved in civic clubs—and pay their dues.

At the Rotary Club, I was following in my father's footsteps. He had been the club's president, and had recently completed a term as district governor for all the Rotary Clubs of Southeastern North Carolina. Of course, I had grown up hearing about Rotary's ethical guidelines and culture of service, which couldn't help but rub off on me and my brothers.

My Rotary dues were $280 a year. DARE's agreement to pay them was especially welcome that first year, because I had decided not to ask for a raise in Year Two. On Nov. 1, 1978, I told the Executive Committee that our budget was painfully tight. One reason was that my assistant director and our part-time secretary had originally been paid from a federal job-creation grant that was expiring. The second reason, I explained, was that "we are slow in raising private sector funds this year."

That was a chronic problem. Often, my economic-development work had to take a back seat to fundraising, just to be sure we could meet payroll and pay the rent.

That December, with our fiscal year half over, I reported to my board that we had spent roughly half of our $89,700 budget. I also lamented, "Raising money is difficult and time-consuming. Taking too great a share of the work load." The solution, I recommended, would be to create a special tax district covering the Central Business District. Property-tax revenue from that district would support DARE, as well as being available for business promotions, beautification, and other purposes specific to downtown.

It was a great idea. Unfortunately, it was way ahead of Wilmington's political realities. Some downtown merchants and landlords loved the idea; others hated it. Wilmington would, eventually, enact that special downtown tax district, but not for another four decades. Long after I had left DARE, the city finally did agree to a recommendation from the renamed Wilmington Downtown, Inc., and established a Municipal Services District. With its seven-cent tax rate per every $100 in property value, this has generated around $375,000 a year to pay for special infrastructure maintenance and cleaning, beautification, economic development work, uniformed downtown "ambassadors" on the street, and targeted marketing. It took effect on July 1, 2017.

But in 1978, money was tight. So in addition to foregoing my own raise, I revised DARE's communication goals, too. We would have to cut back on paid advertising, and put more emphasis on free publicity and promotions. Fortunately, in those days all the significant local news media were interested in what we were doing, and regularly gave us invaluable exposure—news coverage that didn't cost us a dime.

Speaking of payroll: At the end of 1978, I had to make an important staff change. My assistant director, Roger Frankoff, had resigned to take a high-profile planning job in Charleston, S.C. He had been DARE's first employee, on the job even before my

Mary Gornto was the author's top assistant at DARE. She later would become executive director herself.

unfortunate predecessor as executive director. Sorry as I was to lose him, I was pleased to have found an excellent replacement.

Starting work right after New Year's Day 1979 was Mary Murchison Gornto. Her initial job title was community relations director, which revived the concept if not the precise title under which Frankoff had originally been hired. Gornto came from a prominent "Old Wilmington" family, and soon was functioning as DARE's assistant director.

Eventually, after I resigned in 1982, she would succeed me as DARE's top executive. After major achievements downtown, she went on to work as an assistant county manager, then became Wilmington's city manager. Her last job before retiring was as a top administrator at UNC-Wilmington.

Living over the Store

Before getting to our challenges and accomplishments in 1979, I need to go back to the matter of our little $25,000 loan fund. The first handful of loans we made helped finance a couple of small businesses, which would have enormous consequences in the decades to follow. Within a year, the owners of those two businesses would become downtown's very first merchants to live "over the store." From that humble start in two elegant old commercial buildings would begin an explosion of residential development in what had once been a purely commercial downtown. At first, this was mostly in empty upper stories renovated into apartments.

Today, of course, downtown can boast thousands of residential units, many of them in new apartment or condo complexes, but many still in old commercial buildings. As natural as that seems now, it was quite unheard of in the 1970s. Unheard of, that is, until three brave, pioneering business people decided to revive a very old practice.

It wasn't easy, being the first in generations to live over the store. Just combining commercial and residential uses in the same building, in those days, created huge challenges with building codes and building inspections. Appraisers and lenders didn't know how to manage valuations and loans for such hybrid properties. But from DARE's point of view, it was great having people living downtown, present twenty-four/seven. That would enhance many of our other goals. What better way to counter the prejudice that our reviving downtown was unsafe than to point to people who felt comfortable not just visiting, but living there?

Residential pioneers Bob Jenkins and Charles and Nelda Illick were the first to live above their downtown businesses at 12 and 10 Market Street, seen here in the late 1970s.

Those pioneering downtown residents were Charles and Nelda Illick, who ran a print shop known at the time as Postal Instant Press, or PIP Printing; and Bob Jenkins, whose business was interior design. The Illicks' print shop, at 10 Market St., was right next door to Jenkins's interior-design showroom at number 12.

One reason for keeping their business downtown, Charlie Illick said at the time, was that much of PIP's business came from companies with offices nearby. But aside from that, he said, "We like the downtown area."

DARE's involvement began in 1978. We helped the Illicks with financing to buy their building and move PIP into it. Our loan took a "third position," behind two commercial mortgages. That sort of lending was typical of how we operated: Bridging the gaps often left by conventional lenders. The Illicks' total project, by the way, ended up costing $60,000.

Next door, Bob Jenkins was putting $55,000 into his building. In both cases, the owners planned to move in after selling their previous homes in the Historic District.

Starting the following June, while running their business, Charlie and Nelda were also busy rehabilitating 10 Market Street's second floor as their

Nelda and Charles Illick moved their PIP Print shop to 10 Market Street in 1978, and made their home over the store. Along with their next-door neighbor Bob Jenkins and his partner, they were downtown's first modern-day residents.

At 12 Market Street, Bob Jenkins lived above his ground-floor interior design showroom.

A well-known figure with his trademark straw hat and cane, Bob Jenkins led walking tours of downtown and the Historic District after he became one of downtown's first residents.

home. And, not surprisingly, they were also running into trouble with the building inspector.

The issue was a building-code rule that required robust fire-proofing, typically using multiple layers of drywall plasterboard, between commercial and residential spaces. The code's purpose was to protect people in their homes by slowing down the spread of a fire that might begin, unnoticed, in adjacent commercial enterprises. I got involved in October 1979, asking the building inspector to be flexible in how he enforced that rule. Meeting it immediately, by installing additional layers of plasterboard on the print shop's ceiling, would have disrupted PIP's business during the run-up to the Christmas season.

Charlie and Nelda were in a bind. Expecting to move into their over-the-store quarters that month, they had already sold their house in the Historic District. If they couldn't get a break, they would face an impossible choice: Either shut their business down at its busiest time, or wind up with no place to live. So I asked for a short delay in enforcing the fireproofing rule.

I started on this personal note: "The Illicks have been pioneers in promoting commercial and residential development in downtown. They have been very helpful in selling others on doing downtown projects. We need to encourage the Illicks. They have given a lot to the city; we need to give them something in return." Then I offered a practical argument: That the very nature of this live-above-the-store situation made it highly unlikely that a fire in their shop downstairs could burn for a full hour—what the building code rule assumed—without being noticed by the resident owners upstairs.

It was a delicate business, but we made it work. Charlie and Nelda were able to move in, the building code requirements were met, and next door, Bob Jenkins and his partner had also moved in to their second-story apartment. Once both couples were safely in their new homes, I could announce this to the DARE Board.

A newspaper feature about the Illicks and Jenkins got Wilmingtonians thinking for the first time about downtown as a place to live. Jenkins proved an eloquent spokesman. "I have faith that downtown Wilmington will come back," the story quoted him. "Sooner or later, people are going to enjoy the sophistication of this urban area that has a tremendous amount of charm, beauty and character. People will enjoy just being here."

The Illicks' PIP Printing has changed owners over the years, but remains downtown, operating under the name Dock Street Printing. Their former address, 10 Market St., is now a popular French restaurant, Caprice Bistro. Bob Jenkins, of course, would become famous as a tour guide. As colorful an advocate for downtown as we could ever hope to find, Jenkins gained fame as the leader of historic walking tours, heavy on the gossip and dark secrets that surround many of downtown's old buildings. With his straw hat, cane, and endless store of historical anecdotes about downtown and the Historic District, he was a local celebrity and a tourist attraction in his own right for many years. He died in 2018 at the age of 83.

Jenkins' former quarters at 12 Market St. still houses an interior design showroom.

These pioneers' example led to a number of other mixed-use projects over the next several years. Those included multi-unit residential projects at what was called Pontiac Place, in a former car dealership at 311 N. Second St., and The Livery, a former horse stable at 118 Dock St.

Since 1979, downtown Wilmington has never been without full-time residents, more and more of them each year. Turning all those vacant upper-level office spaces into highly coveted apartments was one of DARE's major accomplishments in those crucial early years. The Central Business District wasn't just a place to work; it has also become a great place to live and play.

Public Relations and Public Improvements

When 1979 began, we were keeping a wary eye on construction at Independence Mall. But we were also working toward some other important goals. We hoped these could partly fill the gap that departing retailers would leave. One was to encourage federal offices, then scattered to multiple sites around Wilmington, to consolidate downtown.

Another perennial issue was Wilmington's need for a proper convention center. Every few years, the city's business leaders and politicians had tried to enlist public support for one. One of those years was 1979. But because this would come up once again just during my time with DARE, I'll address it in more detail elsewhere. However, because city and county officials would decline to form a convention center authority that year, DARE kept its focus on more immediately achievable goals.

As they had from the beginning, those included helping landlords restore their buildings' façades and advertising events designed to attract visitors downtown.

During my first year running DARE, I had an advertising and promotion budget of a little over $11,000. That mostly went for print advertising, divided between the daily newspaper and *Cape Fear Scene*, a monthly lifestyle magazine. Instead of the full-blown marketing campaigns we had envisioned, with the costs shared across the entire downtown business community, our slim budget forced us to keep our focus limited. Much of what we spent promoted events, such as a Corvette show we co-sponsored in March 1979, and the Azalea Festival parade the following month.

Public turnout for those was encouraging, especially since we were already planning a brand-new festival, which we hoped would focus public attention on the waterfront.

Meanwhile, fortunately, the merchants of the Downtown Wilmington Association had come up with some money of their own to fund a radio promotion campaign. It was to run from March through May, 1979, with the theme "Rediscover Downtown Wilmington." They offered to share that slogan and a jingle they had developed with any downtown business willing to air its own radio spots. It was a welcome offer. Unfortunately, it wouldn't be repeated; after the mall opened, downtown's remaining merchants would prove unwilling to participate in the joint marketing plans we proposed.

* * *

By far the biggest and most complicated project we worked on that year was an interlocking bundle of public improvements and private investments pulled together under the umbrella of a major federal grant. Wilmington qualified for this, being one of just two cities in North Carolina considered economically "distressed." (The other one was Asheville.) This money was called an Urban Development Action Grant, or UDAG. The city planned to use that for a park and street improvements where Market and Water Streets intersect along the river. That would become our first Riverfront Park and was the beginning of the Riverwalk.

At the same time, I was working to encourage a high-profile private renovation project at the same corner. The three-story brick building at 2 Market Street, known as the Hoggard Building, had been vacant for years. In April, 1979, I shepherding the property through a series of transactions that included a DARE-backed rehabilitation loan, its sale to investors from

Virginia, the rehabilitation work itself, and eventually the opening of a brand-new restaurant.

It may be useful to understand what was involved with such a major rehab job.

The old building's bricks had been painted over. To remove the paint without damaging the masonry, the contractor used chemical means rather than sandblasting. Glass blocks were removed from the window openings and replaced with double-hung sashes. All this, not including any needed interior work, cost $14,346. Factoring for inflation, that was equivalent to more than $70,000 in 2025 dollars.

Renovating the building's façade was one thing. But finding the right tenant was another. That would take some time.

* * *

All the while, Independence Mall got closer and closer to opening. One of its three anchors, the Sears department store, had already opened that spring. But because Sears had moved across the street from its earlier location in Hanover Center (it had left what was now The Cotton Exchange in the early 1960s) that had no immediate impact on downtown. But soon, Aug. 1 would arrive, the rest of the mall would open its doors, and that would be the end of mass retailing in the Central Business District. Belk-Beery and J.C. Penney would close their downtown stores. Several smaller downtown stores would either relocate entirely or open new branches in the mall, while trying to hold on in their original locations, too.

* * *

If there was ever a time to bolster public opinions about downtown, this was it. After DARE's annual meeting in June, we invited all the directors, plus various civic leaders and media people, on a wine-and-cheese cruise. This was on board the tour boat *Captain J.N. Maffitt*, which operated out of Thomas Wright's Chandler's Wharf complex. The invitations called this river tour "an opportunity to view the development activity along Wilmington's waterfront." This impressed the visitors and generated favorable press coverage, as we had hoped.

As my first fiscal year as executive director ended that June, I reported to the Board on what we had accomplished.

For starters, fund-raising in 1978-79 had been "not as strong as the year before." Of $45,000 in private-sector pledges, we actually collected

When Thomas Wright Jr. developed Chandler's Wharf, he also began a river tour service with this boat, the 'Captain J.N. Maffitt,' seen stopping at the Battleship North Carolina's pier. Attracting battleship visitors across the river to the downtown waterfront was one important goal of the new Market Plaza park on the river in front of the federal courthouse.

$42,000. Several of DARE's first-year contributors had declined to help us in our second year, I noted.

On the plus side, "DARE maintained an excellent rapport with the news media in the Wilmington area during fiscal 1978-79," I reported. We had "assisted news people in developing feature stories. DARE never failed to comment or take a position when called upon to do so by the press."

Helping to tell our story, we had published three brochures, including one about our façade renovation loan fund. Another was a reprint of the U.S. secretary of the interior's guidelines for rehabilitating old buildings. The third was a multi-page visitor's guide to downtown.

Then, with the board, I worked out our plan of work for the 1979-80 fiscal year.

Most important was economic development: Not just to recruit new merchants, but to keep as many of the old ones as possible. Specific goals were to "slow down retail flight to suburbs" and "stabilize retail sales," increase public and private investment, increase out-of-town visitation, increase the number of rehab jobs and façade upgrades, and encourage development of more residential units.

That wasn't all. The goals for the year also included getting the springtime Azalea Festival more involved with downtown, creating a summer festival of some kind, and launching the fall festival we hoped would return public attention to the Cape Fear River.

No sooner had we settled on that plan of work than we had to confront City Hall over parking rates. At that time, most on-street parking was free, with a two-hour limit. But a few short-term spaces, for example in front of the Post Office, had meters that took a penny for twelve minutes. City Manager Bob Cobb wanted to raise that short-term rate to a dime for fifteen minutes, while continuing the two-hour free parking elsewhere. He also proposed doubling the fine for overtime parking from $1 to $2.

DARE thought that was a bad idea, even if just from a public-relations standpoint. Just as downtown's retail community was about to take a hit from the mall opening, it would become less convenient to shop downtown. The merchants of the Downtown Wilmington Association opposed the new parking plan, and we did, too. I asked for a meeting with Cobb to explain our opposition to the higher rates "and to ask for better communication between the city and DARE, Inc." This was an early indicator of something that would be a chronic challenge: How to manage our often productive, but sometimes tense, relationship with the city manager.

* * *

But before we could make any headway on any of these issues, we would have to put out another fire. That summer, we got wind of a threat to demolish one of the vacant old Atlantic Coast Line Railroad warehouses along the waterfront, just north of the Cape Fear Technical Institute campus. It had been built in 1888, added to in 1904, and featured large open spaces, bare brickwork, and exposed wooden beams overhead. It was the kind of building that would be treasured in years to come, but wasn't fully appreciated at the time.

What was then a joint city-county Planning Department looped DARE in to its contacts with the state's Historic Preservation Office. While city and state officials were in touch with the railroad's management, offering to help them preserve that and other landmark buildings, I took a different approach.

I approached Thomas Wright, the developer of Chandler's Wharf's, who had both deep pockets and a deep concern for historic preservation. He agreed to my idea: To buy the warehouse from the railroad. But the railroad declined his offer.

The following year, we got the railroad to accept some money to halt its demolition plans, buying time for a rehab project. Part of that deal secured the newly formed Wilmington Railroad Museum a home in the building. It would take a few more years and a lot of work, but eventually a full-blown rehab plan came together.

It was after I had left DARE that my successors finally arranged financing to buy both of the old ACL warehouses, rehabilitate them as a conference center, and help private investors build a new hotel next door, right on the riverfront. Wright, through his Wright Chemical Co., played an important role in all this. DARE got the property, took over the Railroad Museum's existing leases, and eventually completed the meeting facility known as the Coast Line Center.

That finally came together in 1989. By that time, Bob Murphrey had become DARE's executive director. He finished the work I had begun and Mary Gornto had continued. To manage the center, a non-profit called Coast Line Convention Management, Inc. was created. I was hired as its part-time executive director. That job didn't last long, though. By September 1988, before the center even opened, I realized that doing that important job right would take too much time away from my commercial real estate business. So I resigned. Eventually, Bob Murphrey would take the position.

As mentioned earlier, the facility was called a "conference" center because it could accommodate only medium-sized events.

Even with its limitations, it was a major step forward for downtown.

Creating Riverfest: A New Focus on the Cape Fear

In 1979, when this process was just beginning, I had plenty of other pressing concerns. I decided it was time to start getting aggressive about money. In August, I asked for a bigger budget for promotion.

A month later, I asked for a larger loan fund with fewer restrictions, and measures to provide DARE with a "stabilized and equitable sources of operating funds." Well, as I've said, that would have required a special tax district, and that wouldn't happen until well into the Twenty-First Century. But I kept asking!

Meanwhile, on Aug. 1, 1979, Independence Mall had opened. Besides trying to reassure the retailers who hadn't yet bolted to the 'burbs, I had my hands full with a project that would help change public opinion about downtown. With help from partners in the Arts Council and the Residents

Crowds throng the waterfront during the first Riverfest in 1979. Work on Market Plaza and the first stretch of the Riverwalk would transform the foot of Market Street starting in 1981.

of Old Wilmington, I was creating a fall festival focused on the Cape Fear River. Its formal title was the "Old Wilmington Riverfront Celebration." Soon enough, though, it got the name it's had ever since: Riverfest.

Although it wasn't entirely new to have a festival downtown—the Azalea Festival's Saturday-morning parade had been a downtown fixture for a generation—we planned to try something entirely different with Riverfest.

First were the events directly involving the river, notably a raft race. This would become a huge deal, drawing vast crowds of cheering spectators to the waterfront. Dozens of volunteer crews would paddle and pedal a weird, motley assortment of improvised craft through the Cape Fear's tricky tidal currents.

As a venue for live entertainment, we arranged to have a barge moored opposite the Federal Courthouse. It would be a floating stage for musical acts.

Then there was the food. Unlike the Azalea Festival parade, which was always over by noon on Saturday, we hoped Riverfest visitors would stay downtown all day. That meant they would need to eat. And even though downtown's restaurants were delighted with the business they got, they couldn't feed everybody. That first Riverfest featured just two food booths, selling hot dogs and sodas, run by volunteers from two churches. In later years, long rows of professional "carnie" food trailers would take over that role; but in Year 1, those two amateur hot dog stands would have to do.

Maybe the most precedent-busting, in the same year that liquor by the drink was legalized in New Hanover County, we set up the first-ever Riverfest Beer Tent. It may seem quaint today, but in October 1979 it was nothing short of revolutionary for people to hang out downtown on a sunny day, enjoying the river and the sunshine, the crowds and the events, while sipping on a cold beer.

Riverfest's dramatic success got the attention of the long-established Azalea Festival. Soon, that huge April event would also fully embrace downtown, most importantly by emulating the "street fair" approach that Riverfest had pioneered. Instead of leaving downtown deserted once the Saturday-morning parade was over, Azalea Festival crowds now throng Water Street and nearby businesses for a full weekend every spring, just as Riverfest crowds do every autumn.

It's worth a moment to mention two men who would become the public face of Riverfest, its co-chairs in its first year. They were Edwin L. Toone III and Karl V. Sutter, Jr.

Both were retailers. Ed Toone and his wife Bates ran a gift shop in Wilmington's oldest building, at Front and Orange Streets where the Central Business District meets the Historic District. Sutter was one of the very first merchants to move into the Cotton Exchange, where he owned two shops. Together, Toone and Sutter helped begin a tradition that quickly solidified Riverfest's place in Wilmington's calendar of major events.

When the DARE board met the week afterward, the minutes stated, "The recent Riverfest was described as highly successful. Upon acclamation by the board, certificates for outstanding contributions to the revitalization of downtown Wilmington were presented to the co-chairmen of Riverfest '79, Mr. E.L. Toone, III, and Mr. Karl V. Sutter, Jr."

After that meeting, I led the board on a walking tour. I wanted everyone to see, up close, all the properties that we were working on, or hoping to. We started at Cooperative Savings & Loan, where we had just met in the company's boardroom.

We crossed Market Street and walked past the Camera's Eye pornography store, which we were trying to evict from the Diamond Feed Store building on Second Street. We moved on to South Front Street to see a new "Arts Complex" called Bettencourt, which had been developed by Dennis Walsak, a graphic designer and artist. Next stop was Design Workshop, the woodworking business where Jim Nicholson created architectural details for old-building renovations. That space at 9 S. Front St., which had hosted that groundbreaking Halloween party the year before, would eventually become a music venue called Front Street News, and then for many years housed the popular Caffe Phoenix restaurant.

From there, we turned down Market Street to look into Bob Jenkins' interior-design showroom and second-floor apartment and then the Illicks' PIP Printing and apartment. Returning to Front Street, we walked north to Princess Street and the Chambered Nautilus restaurant, which Morgan Kenney had recently opened. At Second and Chestnut Streets, we took a look at the former Belk store, destined to be our new main library, and the Cape Fear Hotel, which was being converted into apartments for the elderly.

The tour returned to North Front Street, where the board saw the insurance office that Glasgow Hicks had relocated into the historic A. David Building. Then we walked up to The Cotton Exchange, which was expanding. We concluded on Third Street, at the Heart of Wilmington hotel. At the time, that hotel was still an important part of the downtown landscape. For example, it was where the Rotary Club met. Now long gone, it occupied the site where Cape Fear Community College's main nursing school building stands.

I mention all this because it's a good indication of just how much progress we had made in just two years. And while many of the businesses that were new in 1979 have long since been replaced by others—that's what busy commercial districts are like, after all—it was important enough to remind the public that even after some merchants had fled to the Mall, many others had decided that downtown was the best place for them.

The next day, Oct. 12, I had a chance to make that point to a lender. Urging William N. Rose, a senior executive at Carolina Savings & Loan, to grant a loan on a South Front Street building, I wrote, "Downtown Wilmington is in a transition period, changing for the better." The tax base downtown was about $40 million the previous year, I noted, and recently completed or current projects would add nearly $16 million to that: "An incredible upward shift in capital investment."

I closed with a list of those projects, which included New Hanover County's brand-new Law Enforcement Center (now the Harrelson Center), the new library, expansions of both The Cotton Exchange and Chandler's Wharf, the Cape Fear Hotel apartment project, and the apartments upstairs from Jenkins' showroom and PIP Printing.

My job involved a lot of that sort of persuasion, not just among the private sector, but also with our backers on the City Council and the Board of County Commissioners.

I was still trying to get the elected officials to endorse the idea of a special tax district. I asked DARE's Executive Committee to pursue it.

"The original thinking" when DARE was created, I told the committee, had been that both public and private sectors would benefit from its work and that both should pay for its operations. The three-year pledges we'd gotten at the beginning had allowed DARE "to prove that it could effectively deal with downtown problems."

In 1979, The Cotton Exchange shopping and dining complex was already expanding, an important boost for downtown when the new Independence Mall was about to open.

We had proved that, I argued, pointing to that twenty-five percent increase in the tax base, which would provide nearly $200,000 in new revenue to the city and county. "A great return," I pointed out, "considering the small investment by both."

But when it came to the business community, I had to be blunt. "Voluntary contributions from the private sector are difficult to secure, unfair and inequitable in size, and non-representative of where the burden of responsibility lies," my memo said. I also mentioned that entirely too much of our staff's time was devoted to fund-raising rather than DARE's "productive work."

My pitch for the special tax district called for a rate of 20 cents on each $100 of valuation on downtown real estate, which would have raised $50,000 in 1980. Adding another $50,000 from the city and $25,000 from the county, in both cases from their general tax revenue, would have given us a budget of $125,000, with no more need for private fund-raising.

I thought my arguments were persuasive. But evidently not persuasive enough. It would be another thirty-eight years before the downtown tax district was finally created.

* * *

The following year, making my annual pitch for funding to the County Commissioners, I offered "An example of a 1980 development project and its impact." This was the W.D. McMillan Building at 107 N. Second St., which had previously housed a resale store—or junk shop—called The Golden Flea. By 1979, the building was empty. It had been condemned and was scheduled for demolition.

I pointed out that the property's tax value, then $31,920, produced $236 in taxes for the dounty that year. If the building was torn down, the vacant lot, valued at $19,000, would have provided the dounty with only $140.60.

To protect its tax base, I urged the county to keep funding DARE so we could keep doing projects like what we had worked out for this building. The lawyer Jerry L. Spivey (he would later get elected as our district attorney) planned to buy, gut and rebuild the former Golden Flea, preserving its historic façade, to become his professional offices. When finished, the building would have a tax value of $108,000, which would produce $827 in tax revenue for the county. "The improvements to the property, which would have been only a vacant lot, will result in an additional $591 in revenue for the county, or nearly $6,000 in the next ten years," I projected.

That building, by the way, now houses the Quanto Basta Italian restaurant.

* * *

Regardless of our perennial budget struggles, DARE was still getting things done. And I kept trying to get better economic data to help our work.

One need was to find better numbers on sales tax collections, narrowed just to the Central Business District. The state Department of Revenue hadn't been especially helpful, so in November 1979 I appealed for help to one of our two state representatives. He just happened to be my father! I maintained all the proprieties; I addressed my letter to "Dear Representative Merritt," rather than "Dear Dad."

Based on such data as we had been able to acquire, in December I could predict that downtown would eventually comprise twenty-five percent restaurants and entertainment businesses and twenty percent residential, with the rest a mix of retail, offices, and government functions. To help that happen, I told DARE's Executive Committee, I would be meeting with the building inspector's office to discuss how we could smooth the way for more residential development in the Central Business District.

At that same December meeting, I ticked off a summary of recent business development, which included eight new businesses in the Cotton Exchange, for a net gain of six; and six new retailers in Chandler's Wharf. On Front Street, I contrasted thirteen new businesses with eight losses. The biggest loss there was J.C. Penney, which had moved to Independence Mall. On Market Street, thanks to the city's proposed urban development project, work on the waterfront park was expected to start in the coming year. The renovation of the old Hoggard Building, to become the Fish Market Restaurant, was expected to proceed in parallel with that work.

Numbers were similar elsewhere. On Princess Street, we had gained eight businesses and lost four; on Second, we'd gained three and lost two, including a very big one: The Belk department store.

But one of those "lost" businesses on Second Street was the Camera's Eye, the "adult book store," whose building had been sold out from under it. We considered that a net positive.

Looking ahead, I elaborated on several other projects, some of which the board had seen during our walking tour in October.

On Front Street, the old Bank of North Carolina building was stripping off an ugly false front and would be restoring a Nineteenth-Century façade. That building, at Front and Princess Streets, now houses the Bourbon Street restaurant, plus apartments on the upper floors.

In the same block, the Foy-Roe clothing store was planning both interior and façade renovations. Its owner commented that the work cost only half of what a year's rent at Independence Mall would have run. That building now houses Front Street Brewery. A few doors up at Number 23, what's known as the Ironfront Building because of its architecturally significant Victorian cast-iron façade was to begin major renovation work in early 1980. Two blocks farther north, Glasgow Hicks was restoring the former A. David building's interior and façade for his insurance office.

On South Front, Dennis Walsak's Bettencourt Arts Complex would be undergoing façade and interior renovations. Next door, the former Barefoots & Jackson furniture store would be renovated to provide office space for the Army Corps of Engineers.

Chandler's Wharf, with its riverfront restaurants, has been downtown Wilmington's southern 'anchor' since the 1970s. The Riverwalk was extended to this point in the 1990s.

Partial façade renovations were also planned on four other buildings, including two at the intersection of Front and Market Streets: Finkelstein's Jewelry & Pawn and Toms Drug Store. Exterior design for the Toms store was by Bob Jenkins, who now lived and worked just down the block.

Finally, Cooperative Savings & Loan was expanding its offices into a Second Street building adjacent to its Market Street headquarters.

We closed out 1979 with yet another new promotional event, called "Downtown Wilmington Candlelight Christmas."

A Grant, a Park, and Lots of Private Investment

Maybe the best news we got as that year came to an end was that the City of Wilmington had received that major federal UDAG grant, which was intended to redevelop the first block of Market Street. By the time the project reached its final form, it included a full block each on North Water Street and Market Street. It would create a park, including the beginning of the Riverwalk.

The full financial package was complex. It combined several different federal loans with local resources, including DARE's façade-rehab loan fund, for a total of a little more than $2 million in public money, plus essential private investment.

Those private dollars would be leveraged by twenty-year loans at generous three-percent interest rates. We lined up nineteen individuals or

When the Belk-Beery department store moved to Independence Mall in 1979, New Hanover County bought Belk's downtown building and converted it into the main public library. The library operated here from 1981 until 2025, when it moved into a brand-new building in the same block.

private firms that would execute commercial rehab contracts under this program. DARE credited this package for "512 new job opportunities." While many were temporary construction jobs, 146 of them were permanent positions for people with low to moderate incomes.

At one point, we calculated that all this, from various governmental and private sources, had created more than $15 million in investments. These included the northward extension of Thomas Wright's Chandler Wharf complex, at $4.5 million, and the county's conversion of the Belk department store as our new main library, at $2.3 million.

It had been tough getting this started. Because the UDAG money was meant to be "leverage" for private investments, the project's scale kept fluctuating as we found private partners—and as some of them dropped out. That meant the scope of the work on Water and

Among the downtown buildings that were renovated with financing arranged through DARE was the Foy-Roe clothing store on North Front Street. Since the 1990s, this building has been home to a popular restaurant, the Front Street Brewery.

Market Streets would keep changing, almost right up until construction began.

A major feature in the April 15 *Sunday Star-News* described the proposed park: "This plaza, in the area where the Fire Department now berths its fireboat, and the U.S. Customs Service keeps confiscated marijuana-smuggling vessels, is intended as a 'welcome center' for visitors first arriving downtown." That, in a nutshell, summarizes the difference between the waterfront as it was, and what we hoped it would become.

Even after some of the proposed investment failed to materialize, the whole package still exceeded $9 million—equivalent to $44 million today. It would go far to kick-start downtown's revitalization.

A key private component of this was one major investment, right at the corner of Market and Water Streets. I've already mentioned the Hoggard Building, which had been vacant for years. Once DARE helped new owners make exterior renovations, it attracted an entrepreneur who understood the appeal of dining in a nicely restored historical structure. His name was Ray Giovannoni. He ran a successful restaurant, called The Fish Market, in the Old Town Alexandria neighborhood just outside Washington, D.C.

He invested in major improvements to the Hoggard Building and, in 1980, opened his second Fish Market location, right in the historic heart of downtown Wilmington. Among his innovations: He built little balconies, each suitable for a table for two, outside his second-story windows. As soon as he opened for business, diners began discovering the charms of eating dinner with a view of the setting sun over the Cape Fear River.

Along with a few other pioneering businesses around the foot of Market Street, the Fish Market and the adjacent park quickly proved to be a central anchor for downtown business, midway between the previously developed Cotton Exchange and Chandler's Wharf.

This was shaping up as something to brag about. At our June 1980 board meeting, I reported that the UDAG grant was being matched with private money from eighteen different entities. Of the $5.2 million that would be invested in a wide range of business properties, $4.7 million was coming from private investors. That was in addition to $800,000 to be used on the waterfront park along Market and Water Streets. We had another $400,000 grant request pending, hoping to enlarge the scope of that project.

And then came a moment to show off the most prominent of the many private investments in the UDAG package. When that busy meeting broke up, I invited the Board to attend the Fish Market Restaurant's opening reception.

Pleased as I was to see that addition to downtown's dining scene, the Fish Market would present some challenges for me personally. One of those tested my self-discipline and ability to steer a course between necessary truth and undiplomatic bluntness. That sensitive moment came in July 1980.

A month after it opened, the Fish Market's general manager asked me what his customers really thought about the place. This called for telling the truth, even though that truth might be far from welcome.

I replied, carefully, in writing. I started off with a summary of the good points: "The Fish Market is a fun and exciting place to be." I cited the "Excellent renovation, good location, satisfactory parking, appealing atmosphere, fun experience." I noted that the nightly entertainment had been "consistently good." But then I had to get to the negative.

"The food is generally no good," I had to tell him. "People enjoy going to the restaurant in general; but they often leave dissatisfied due to poor food and weak service." I warned, "some basic changes must be made in the manner food is prepared and served."

I explained that our local diners expected better from a seafood restaurant. "Wilmington is a seaport town," I wrote, "whose people know the difference between good seafood and bad. In general, the quality of the preparation of the seafood served . . . is not competitive with other restaurants."

It's hard to say whether that bit of "tough love" made much difference. It might have actually hurt our endless fund-raising efforts.

The following April, I sent a letter to the Fish Market's owner, Ray Giovannoni, in Alexandria, Va. "Your restaurant is an important asset for downtown Wilmington and I hope things continue to improve for you," I began. Then I got down to business. "Also, I would like to remind you that we were looking for your decision on the matter regarding the supposedly pledged $400 to DARE for this past year. We would appreciate your support this year and the following year. Contributions are voluntary, but we really do need your help."

That was an example of the chronic problem that I dealt with throughout my time at DARE, and that my successors struggled with, too: Lacking any guaranteed funding source, how could we get the private interests who benefitted from our work to help cover some of its cost?

Renovated with financial help from DARE, the Fish Market Restaurant featured balconies that allowed for open-air dining with a river view. At Market and Water streets, it later became Roy's Riverboat Landing. It is still a popular dining spot, now called Floriana.

Then, during construction of the waterfront park project that had made all these nearby developments possible, Giovannoni started raising Cain with the city. Because of the necessarily disruptive nature of the work, which included rebuilding some buried utility lines, he blamed the project for hurting his restaurant's business. While none of that was under DARE's control, we still had to navigate some of the fallout, including negative publicity about our big project.

Regardless of its owner's attitude or his support for us, the Fish Market continued to attract diners. That was largely because of its location right by the river. The building boasted intimate balconies that provided parties of two with a beautiful view. But eventually its out-of-town owner would sell out to the local restaurateurs Roy and Ann Marie Clifton. They had earlier started a highly successful lunch place, called the Sandwich Factory, on Princess Street. The Fish Market was renamed Roy's Riverboat Landing, and under its new owners it would remain a favorite dining spot for decades to come. Today, a dozen years after Roy Clifton's death, the place is still a restaurant, known as Floriana.

* * *

In August 1980, the city secured the extra $400,000 in federal money it needed to complete the whole waterfront park project as planned. At the time, we expected work to begin in October, right after the second-ever Riverfest.

As it turned out, it wouldn't be until April 1981 that construction started. By then, the project was being called Market Plaza. The expectation was that all but landscaping would be finished before the next Riverfest. Soon, pavement was torn up on Market and Water Streets, utilities were excavated, and for a time the heart of our riverfront was a construction zone. And despite complaints from one or two Market Street merchants, the work proceeded well.

It would be early 1982 when Market Plaza—which later would become the center of the Riverwalk and site of the city's main visitor center—was finally finished. The work transformed downtown's center. It created a central median and ornamental crosswalks in Market Street's first block, to which a historic fountain was returned after being in storage for decades. The project planted trees along its sidewalks. It built a wharf for use by tour boats and river taxis. It replaced Water Street's asphalt pavement with brick. It created an attractive park, with a children's play areas and a riverside promenade, directly opposite the historic Federal Courthouse. As the $1.1 million centerpiece to the Urban Development Action Grant project, it had been meant to encourage private development. By the time it opened, it had already paid off. That project would continue to pay dividends for decades to come.

Evicting the 'Adult' Establishments

Among the most vexing problems in those early years were the so-called "adult" businesses. Besides making downtown unattractive to most visitors, they were also a focus for crime, especially prostitution. And, as I discovered when I started getting threats on my life, many of them were run by organized crime groups.

Already, by the end of 1979, we had seen one of the porn shops, The Camera's Eye, put out of business when its building was sold. That set an excellent precedent for what to do about the rest of them.

The heart of downtown: Where DARE and the City of Wilmington concentrated their early efforts, building Market Plaza park on Market Street and in front of the U.S. courthouse. This view also shows the restaurant originally known as the Fish Market, the city's main visitor center, and at right the J.W. Brooks Building, which the author would renovate.

Eventually, DARE settled on a dual strategy to get rid of all the "adult" businesses and then keep new porn shops and stripper bars from opening nearby.

For the first half of that plan, we relied on the public spirit and substantial bank accounts of Thomas H. Wright, Jr. While Chandler's Wharf was his most visible contribution to a revitalized downtown, I can't say enough about the vital additional help he gave us behind the scenes, toward this and other important objectives. He's a great example of how a Citizen Warrior can use his own resources for the greater good. Although he developed Chandler's Wharf as a business venture, his direct and badly needed financial help to DARE didn't seem to be motivated by anything more than a desire to improve his home town.

On Feb. 12, 1980, I reported to DARE's Executive Committee that we were preparing to buy the Ahrens Building at 112 Market St. Its tenant was The Palace, a bar that featured bare-breasted dancers. DARE was able to make that purchase thanks to Wright's guarantee of our loan. Our first purpose, I told the committee, was to evict the tenant. Then, we meant to spruce up the building, fix roof leaks and otherwise ensure it was weatherproof, and possibly renovate its façade to make it more attractive to investors. And when we found someone willing to redevelop the building, we would sell it with restrictive covenants. Those covenants would bar any future owners from renting to so-called "adult" establishments.

During this delicate phase, we decided that it was best to keep Wright's role quiet, lest other landlords start demanding higher prices. A couple of months later, after successfully completing the purchase, the DARE board approved a motion of "official thanks to the anonymous backer who aided in the purchase of this building." So while our Executive Committee knew Wright's identity, neither our full board nor the public did.

In July 1980, after I'd presented an update on the Ahrens Building and The Palace bar, the Executive Committee asked me to prepare a similar package for another building in the same block of Market Street. At the same time, we considered leasing a building on South Front at Dock, which housed an "adult" bookstore, although it would end up being demolished after a botched renovation attempt by its owners.

Soon we repeated the process, spending $24,000 to buy 114 S. Front St. so we could evict the Friendly Lounge. Once again, Tom Wright stepped up to guarantee the loan. He also promised to buy the property from DARE if we couldn't find another buyer.

Several times, we extended our buy-out strategy to buildings whose tenants weren't explicitly sex-oriented, but still contributed to a "skid row" atmosphere. One of those was the Advance Building at 16 S. Front St. In early 1981, it was occupied by a disco and lounge. DARE bought and resold it. For many years now, it has housed the popular Nikki's Fresh Gourmet and Sushi.

Our second strategy in attacking the stripper bars and porn shops was to get a "dispersal" amendment added to Wilmington's zoning code. In early 1979, DARE's attorney, Bill Shell, had begun researching how zoning might restrict so-called "adult" businesses. By March, I reported to the Board, Shell was prepared to draft just such an amendment to Wilmington's zoning rules. This prohibited any so-called "adult entertainment" business from operating within 300 feet of any other similar business—or any church or school.

That ensured that as we bought up the buildings, evicted their troublesome tenants, and sold them off with restrictive covenants, no "adult" business could come right back and open up shop next door. The result of the zoning change was that porn shops and stripper bars could legally operate in only a handful of tracts scattered around the city, none of them anywhere near downtown. And so, within a year or so, we had eliminated most of these types of businesses. Our strategy had been a great success and had given new hope to downtown.

* * *

By early 1979, even before the mass merchandisers left for Independence Mall, we were already seeing other reasons for optimism. For one thing, the two new shopping-and-dining developments in old historic buildings, The Cotton Exchange on the north and Chandler's Wharf on the south, were beginning to function as anchors to downtown. That was very much like how the big department stores were anchors for smaller retailers at the mall: Destinations for shoppers who would then discover the many other, smaller establishments nearby. Already, these two downtown projects were attracting out-of-town visitors. And already, we were hoping that a major surge in tourist trade would come, taking up the slack from the impending departure of traditional retailers.

One key to attracting visitors, of course, was making it easy to get around. The Transit Authority's free shuttle bus was a helpful step. But we still had challenges with traffic circulation and parking.

The pre-DARE city project that had turned a block of North Front Street into a "pedestrian mall" was still making it tricky to get around. In late 1978, in response to our pleas, the City Council had ordered that the street fronting The Cotton Exchange be reopened to traffic. Engineers warned that its ornamental brick and stone pavement, designed for foot traffic, wouldn't hold up under vehicle tires. But a quickie job to repave the block stalled. It would eventually be rolled into a much bigger project to redevelop several other blocks of North Front. The city's proposal was to restore two-way traffic to what had been a single-lane one-way street and replace angle parking with parallel parking. That's how it remains to this day.

Spreading the Word, and Some Blunt Words

Most of our work in those early years, in close coordination with the city government, involved leveraging public funding to encourage private investment. Besides the major UDAG package, lower-profile but essential work included seeking federal Small Business Administration loans to help new businesses to get started or to help established ones to improve their properties.

Even before the UDAG project got under way, the public was taking notice.

When the *Sunday Star-News* published its 1980 "Progress" supplement, the editor Charles "Andy" Anderson offered this comment about downtown: "More and more professional and business people have found it a unique and inviting location. Sometime early in this decade some $6 million will be spent by private enterprise and through government grants to develop one of its great resources: The waterfront."

That annual business-review section reported that downtown property values were beginning to rise again, despite the previous year's departure of most major retailers. It noted that several important commercial blocks now had new or relocated businesses in formerly vacant storefronts, that New Hanover County was converting the old Belk store into a library, and that at least one landmark downtown office building was being renovated.

That article acknowledged, though, that DARE was "still struggling to find developers for remaining large, empty buildings," and that the city government was searching for enough money to complete its ambitious plans to rebuild downtown's streets and public areas.

* * *

In April 1980, DARE's long-range planning committee listed goals that included increasing downtown's employment numbers from 4,500, which reflected the exodus of the two big department stores, to 6,500 to 7,000 people by 1990. The committee charged us—the staff—with maintaining and developing office space, with a secondary emphasis on residential growth, "particularly on the upper floors of commercial structures."

Other "areas of interest" the committee mentioned were recreation and entertainment, a civic/convention center, and continued development along the waterfront.

To meet those goals, I told the DARE Board in June, I would need a more robust promotion and advertising program, and a budget to pay for it. I suggested pulling the various merchant groups together, with at-large help from a banker, an insurance person, and a lawyer, to coordinate advertising for downtown businesses. DARE itself, I proposed, should limit our ad buys to "only to those directly related to the economic development of downtown."

Our proposal for a joint advertising effort immediately ran into a familiar obstacle: The downtown merchants' reluctance to participate. Mary Gornto wrote to the various merchants' groups, proposing a sit-down to discuss our idea of a joint council to manage promotion and advertising. The

Downtown Wilmington Association sent back a sharp note. That biggest of the merchants' groups "will not be represented at this meeting and will not be participating in the proposed program," its president, Vernon Teague, declared. He didn't even bother to explain his group's objections to the idea.

Undeterred, though, our PR Committee would forge ahead. For 1980-81, it included an advertising sales representative from the *Morning Star*, the general manager of one of Wilmington's two TV stations, an executive from a group of local radio stations, and the irrepressible Bob Jenkins.

For the 1980-81 fiscal year, I asked for $7,000, plus private-sector money enough to hire a part-time employee to manage business promotions, advertising, and "business education." That last category included such things as "business practices" and "regulation of hours," as well as safety, sanitation, and communications.

At the same June 1980 meeting, our Promotion & Public Relations Committee reported that the "tremendous success" of Riverfest in attracting people downtown had encouraged it to sponsor other events: The Candlelight Christmas in December and an antique car show, under the umbrella title of "Preservation Week," in May. Both had seemed promising. Turnout for both, unfortunately, had proved disappointing.

Those events had been only moderately successful, partly because of a lack of support and involvement from the merchants. Delivering the PR Committee's report, Mary Gornto told the board, "I do believe that most such events should be developed by the merchants."

She pointed out that while Riverfest had been originated by DARE, with help from a couple of organizations, it had already become an independent, non-profit corporation. And so, after just a year, DARE had gotten out of the event business.

Because of that experience, we decided, the coming year's emphasis should be on general public relations and economic development advertising, "and not on specific promotions."

Two ways we aimed to carry out that goal were to publish 30,000 copies of *A Visitors Guide to Historic Downtown Wilmington*, (later bumped up to a 50,000 press run) and working with *Tarheel Magazine* on a twenty-page supplement to its June 1980 issue. We would get 15,000 copies of that to distribute.

In another approach to public relations, we were busy spreading our message to civic and professional organizations. That year, I gave speeches to ten groups, including Optimist and Civitan clubs, the American Association of University Women, and the Residents of Old Wilmington. Mary Gornto gave four speeches, to Civitans, the Colonial Dames, the Sons of the American Revolution, and the Historic Preservation Society of North Carolina.

* * *

From time to time, like when expressing myself a bit too freely about a powerful state legislator got me fired from the State Ports Authority, I have given in to the temptation to speak bluntly. During my time at DARE, I sometimes played a "bad cop" role, which let me take the heat for taking positions that rubbed people the wrong way. This happened a couple of times in the summer of 1980. I've already mentioned how I told a new restaurant's manager that his food was "no good." Then, in the course of negotiations with the city government about its financial contribution to DARE, I wrote an intemperate letter to City Manager Bob Cobb. After I cooled off, I apologized to him and to two of his top assistants.

I suppose it's inevitable: Sometimes, when taking an important stand, it's impossible to avoid giving offense. But even so, it's important to be personally humble and admit a mistake. The objective should always be more important than the ego.

As my brother John has said: "There are no permanent allies, just permanent causes."

Such bumps in the road aside, our progress was steady during 1980.

In August, I reported that we had made loans totaling $46,000 (almost all of the available $49,000) from our façade renovation fund, and $5,000 had already been repaid.

During the second annual Riverfest, on Oct. 4, DARE held an open house, which we billed under the name "To Progress." Posters displayed in downtown businesses invited Riverfest attendees to visit six different projects we were supporting. Those included the Cape Fear Hotel Apartments and the future public library on Chestnut Street; the new law offices in what had been the Golden Flea building on Second Street; the Trust Building at Front and Market Streets; the Joseph Harper Walker Building on South Water Street; and the Beddingfield & Jordan Building on South Front.

In the spring of 1981, while waiting for construction on the waterfront park to commence, we had an opportunity to showcase our accomplishments to peers from other cities. The previous summer, I had been elected to the

Board of Directors of the International Downtown Executives Association (IDEA) as well as president of the North Carolina Downtown Development Association.

Those positions helped me steer IDEA's Executive Development Institute to Wilmington in April. It was gratifying to be able to show off some of our early successes to my professional peers from other cities. I like to think that some of them were inspired by our example; I certainly got some great ideas from that same round of meetings.

Plenty of other issues kept us busy, including parking, promotion, and public relations. Despite the limited funds we had available for P.R., we had reasons for satisfaction. According to a June, 1981 report to the board, "Extensive publicity has been on-going throughout the year, resulting both from news releases and from media-initiated coverage."

As much as anything, we concluded, Riverfest had helped tell downtown's story. As I told the board, it had been "highly successful in attracting people to the area, where they have fun and become aware of the changes taking place."

In my June 1981 "State of Downtown Wilmington" report, I contrasted the years from 1970 to 1977, when "virtually no development had taken place in the Central Business District," with the time since DARE had begun. In the four years since 1977, more than $2 million had been invested downtown "and more is planned. The tax base has been stabilized and employment has been reasonably stabilized. Old and historic buildings have been adaptively developed and preserved. Things are clearly looking better. However, there is still much to be done. While we have won some important battles, the war is still raging."

Pressure from suburban developers continued to drain away downtown retail and offices, I said. Then I turned my attention to a group that should have been our closest allies:

"Downtown property owners, as a whole, are not acting responsibly in trying to promote their property to its highest and best usages. Many downtown merchants are not promoting and merchandising effectively. In virtually all cases, the parties involved are afraid to spend money or to take a chance."

I had returned to the blunt talk. My report scolded downtown property owners: "Lack of maintenance is a serious problem."

I scolded downtown business owners: "Up-to-date methods of management must be employed. Aesthetics of store fronts and inside stores need to be improved." Also, I said, those merchants "must better understand the nature of the downtown market," and take such common-sense steps as keeping their stores open during lunchtimes, when people who worked downtown had time to shop.

Finally, I scolded those downtown employees: "Employers must make certain that they and their employees do not park in on-street spaces." Too often in those days, shoppers found no convenient place to park because the spaces nearest the stores were occupied by people who worked downtown.

I also warned that land speculation was discouraging development. (That was an important reason why we hadn't publicized Thomas Wright's financial backing for some of our real estate deals.)

After itemizing the individual buildings DARE had bought, I suggested upping our game. "Now it is time to work on blocks and sections, and/or specific total building developments."

For the coming 1981-82 fiscal year, I proposed that DARE concentrate on finding responsible developers, soliciting new business, and providing technical assistance to existing businesses that wanted to expand. This was no radical departure; just a reiteration of the importance of what we were already doing.

I ended with a long list of goals for our local governments. Once again, City Manager Bob Cobb was my chief target. The City of Wilmington, I said, "Should generally be more cooperative with DARE," and "Should properly maintain the streets and public spaces downtown, including the Front Street Mall" next to The Cotton Exchange. "Without the cooperation of the city administration," I warned, "some of DARE's efforts will be endangered."

Both city and county, I said, should offer more of their limited parking spaces to the general public, rather than reserving them for their own employees.

I closed with a goal for the state of North Carolina: Complete our region's most badly needed highway projects, beginning with Interstate 40. But that particular crusade is a story for another chapter.

It wasn't surprising that this ruffled some feathers. Not surprisingly, Bob Cobb wasn't pleased. And publicity about my "state of downtown" report led two merchants to resign from the DARE Board. They were Ann

Finkelstein, whose business at South Front and Market Streets combined a jewelry and music store with a pawn shop, and Albert F. Rhodes, who owned a jewelry business. I was sorry to lose them, but I believed I had a duty to tell the truth, however unwelcome.

Much of our truth, however, was both positive and encouraging. In our annual report, I summarized the accomplishments of 1980-81. We had helped twelve businesses to set up shop downtown. We had re-sold the first of the buildings we had bought, and had put the second on the market. We had saved two businesses that had considered leaving downtown, although two others had left; a fifth was still undecided. We had made five façade renovation loans for $23,700, contributing to rehab work valued at $193,000. We had helped thirteen parties get loans. We had reprinted our visitors guide and distributed 50,000 copies.

But we weren't entirely in control of our agenda. In September 1981, we—meaning DARE, the city, and downtown's business community—were thrown for a loop. Because of design flaws that had led to cracks in concrete support beams, the old waterfront parking deck was declared unsafe. The city shut it down. While I would have preferred to see the damaged deck demolished and replaced with a more efficient, modern structure, the dire immediate parking shortage dictated a shorter-term expedient. At considerable cost—almost a quarter million—the city decided to reinforce the old structure and extend its useful life. It would remain in place until the early 2000s, bridging the gap until newer, better parking garages could be built elsewhere downtown.

But already in 1981, some of us were seeing the old deck as more of a liability than an asset. It separated the businesses on Front Street from the river. It was occupying a much larger real-estate footprint than its value, or its number of parking spaces, justified. Its capacity was inadequate to meet downtown's growing parking needs, and it couldn't feasibly be converted into a denser, better-designed parking garage without starting from scratch.

It would be another two decades, though, before I was able—as a private developer—to begin replacing it with the first of the mixed-use projects that have finally transformed its site. I will briefly touch on that in a later chapter.

After many failed attempts over the decades to build a facility for large meetings on the downtown riverfront, the Wilmington Convention Center finally opened in 2010.

The Convention Center that Wasn't

Well before DARE got started, the city government had commissioned feasibility studies about needed public facilities. What we inherited from those was a 1974 consultant's report. Its key finding was "that the Wilmington-New Hanover County area requires, and can generate satisfactory support for, a combination arena-exhibit hall complex." The consultants, Hammer, Siler George Associates of Washington, D.C., also recommended "that the facility should be placed, if at all possible, in downtown Wilmington," where it would operate most successfully "while at the same time helping to breathe new life into that area."

Needless to say, DARE agreed with that conclusion. Although UNC-Wilmington's completion of Trask Coliseum in 1977 had largely addressed the "arena" portion of the consultants' recommendation, the city still lacked a suitable venue for large meetings and trade shows.

In March 1979, I reported to our board that the Chamber of Commerce intended to ask the city and county governments to form a convention center authority and to plan for a downtown location. We agreed with that idea, too.

But those ideas would prove to be ahead of their time. We knew it would be an uphill fight to get Wilmington's voters to shoulder a convention center's cost. And even though my successors at DARE in the late 1980s would help get a mini-version developed—it would be called a "conference center" because of its modest capacity—it wouldn't be until a decade into the next century that the actual, full-scale Wilmington Convention Center finally opened its doors.

And so after our local elected officials chose not to form the authority, and with more immediate needs to address, DARE left the convention center report on the shelf.

More than two years later, we had a new report to consider. That important development came in January 1982, with the release of a "location and feasibility analysis" for a convention center. The Chicago consulting firm Real Estate Research declared, "Our research demonstrates the need for additional convention and exhibition space in Wilmington and quantified a strong measure of support for these kinds of facilities."

The consultants said the best site would be the block bounded by Grace, Front, Walnut and Second Streets.

The City Council accepted that report; DARE endorsed it. In May, the city government paid $45,000 to a Washington, D.C. firm for preliminary design work. The basic rough-draft design was to be finished in August, in time for public comment and revision before voters decided a bond referendum in November. DARE, along with the Chamber of Commerce and other tourism-related entities, pushed this proposal, and used the just-completed market analysis as ammunition. The consultants had concluded that a downtown convention center could work if it had a new hotel nearby. (That site the study recommended happens, today, to include a hotel built in the early Twenty-first Century.)

To my acute disappointment, in November 1982 Wilmington's voters returned a resounding "no sale" verdict. The bond issue to finance the convention center had been defeated.

It would be almost three more decades before Wilmington finally got its Convention Center. It opened in November 2010, on the waterfront, though without its adjoining hotel. That would takes years more to get built. The Embassy Suites finally opened in 2018.

The land where that center now operates is the exact site that in 1981 and 1982 had been proposed for a coal-exporting terminal. What happened, and why we have a convention center and not a heap of coal on our riverfront, is a story I'll tell in a later chapter.

A New Career and New Causes

By January of 1982, I had decided it was time for somebody new to take the reins at DARE. I submitted my resignation, effective June 30. Fortunately, I had an outstanding assistant, Mary Gornto. For several years, she and I had worked together as a smooth-running team. I played the "negative" leadership role by bringing important issues to the forefront, fighting as necessary to get them implemented, and serving as a lightning rod for our critics. Mary was our "good cop," serving as public spokesperson for all our efforts. Of course, she had a lot of good and creative ideas herself. With deep roots in "Old Wilmington" society, she was also excellent at establishing personal business relationships. So she was a natural as my replacement.

Those attributes proved themselves in Gornto's subsequent career. After running DARE, she became an assistant New Hanover County manager, then Wilmington's city manager, and finally vice-chancellor for advancement at UNC-Wilmington.

As for me, I was glad to be able to hand over the controls. By the end of four years, I was feeling "burned out." More important, I had also just become a father; my son was born in 1981. It was time to go into business for myself and make better money for my family than a publicly funded entity like DARE could pay. With my background in marketing and communications, I felt that I could do well for myself by returning to that arena.

I left several important projects in Gornto's hands. One of those was the early, and ultimately unsuccessful, attempt to build a proper convention center. She would go on to do much of the important work of creating the smaller, interim Coast Line Center, which opened in 1986. Also about to come to fruition were two outstanding tourism businesses. Carl Marshburn of Cape Fear Riverboats was about to bring the paddle-wheel riverboat *Henrietta II* to the Cape Far River, and John Pucci of Springbrook Farms began horse-drawn carriage tours along the streets of downtown and the Historic District.

The record of accomplishments that began during my final year at DARE included the relocation of eight different government agencies that over the years had leased office space all over town. In answer to a federal mandate, by the end of 1982 most were back downtown in the newly renovated Efird's Department Store building at North Front and Grace Streets.

Also, after the successful completion of the Market Plaza project, the city was extending its medians, decorative crosswalks, and canopy of street trees up Market Street to Second Street, a project that would be complete in 1983.

So I could look back on four productive years. Had I accomplished everything I'd hoped for?

No. Disappointments from DARE's first four years included our failure to get a special tax district created, to establish a cooperative advertising campaign, or to get a convention center built.

But our successes were huge. We had stabilized the downtown tax base after the mass retailers' exodus to the mall. We had leveraged tax incentives and building-code revisions to encourage landlords to strip ugly "modern" façades off historic commercial buildings, transforming downtown's appearance for the better. We had packaged major private investments to match federal grants, both to spruce up private properties and to transform the heart of the Cape Fear Riverfront. We had helped creative restaurateurs demonstrate that diners would flock to places that offered views of the river. We had driven away the sleazy, sex-oriented businesses that had blighted downtown for so many years. We had recruited new businesses that were filling formerly vacant storefronts. We had launched Riverfest, the festival that proved that downtown and the waterfront were important attractions for locals as well as tourists. We had encouraged the beginnings of a residential renaissance on the upper floors of commercial buildings. We had begun to change public attitudes about downtown as a safe, entertaining place to go.

DARE still had lots of work to do, and that work goes on today under the name Wilmington Downtown, Inc. My successors as executive director—Mary Gornto, Bob Murphrey, Susi Hamilton, John Hinnant, and Ed Wolverton among them—all did important work to build on what we accomplished in those first few years. Christina Haley is its chief executive today.

We have our long-awaited Convention Center and several new hotels. Important new buildings have taken the place of the old riverfront parking deck. Tax proceeds from downtown's Municipal Services District are bolstering downtown's safety and attractiveness. Downtown Wilmington is a major tourist attraction in its own right. Excellent restaurants, many of them along the Cape Fear River, offer fine dining, charming settings, and often gorgeous river views. And hundreds of apartments and condominiums, in both new buildings and old, have made downtown one of the city's most sought-after and densely populated neighborhoods.

In my later career as a real estate developer and investor, I helped bring several important downtown projects to fruition. But the market conditions that allowed those developments to exist were largely the result of what DARE and our allies struggled to accomplish all those years ago. I couldn't be prouder than to have been present at the creation.

* * *

Perhaps the best way to wrap up the four years that I ran DARE is to look at its position in early 1983, after a city councilman had proposed establishing a new economic development department. Even without me and my big mouth, DARE minced no words in its response.

"Wilmington must create *pro-development attitude,* not a Development Department," DARE told the Council. That statement cited two examples of the city's negatives: "Recent developers/investors discouraged by City Staff and community attitude." By "community attitude," they meant Wilmington's "No" vote on the convention center and New Hanover County voters' rejection of a countywide water and sewer system. Both those initiatives would take years more to reach fruition. A county sewer system—without a parallel water utility—wouldn't begin until the late 1980s. It would take decades more before the duplicative city and county utility systems would be merged. And while the small, stop-gap Coast Line "conference center" would also get developed during the '80s, Wilmington wouldn't have a facility able to accommodate large-scale events until 2010.

In October 1983, something called the Mayor's Economic Development Task Force issued a report. Its members included Mary Gornto from DARE, Joe Augustine from the Chamber of Commerce, and a couple of city planners. The task force recommended enhancing tourism by establishing "a highly visible, centrally located visitor information center." It suggested the new Market Plaza and the Old Courthouse on Third Street as possible locations. As it turned out, both sites would eventually be established: A staffed information booth in the waterfront park, and the Convention & Visitors Bureau's main offices in the Old Courthouse.

Many of that task force's other recommendations would also come true, but only after many more years. Those included creating the new authority that finally got our Convention Center built and improving the riverfront's appearance as seen from the west, to "invite" visitors to the Battleship North Carolina to come across the river to downtown.

* * *

Three years after I left DARE, Mary Gornto had gone to work for New Hanover County and Bob Murphrey was DARE's executive director.

Meanwhile, I was working on various private projects downtown. At the July 1985, Executive Committee meeting, I was asked to help DARE tackle the only partially resolved issue of disreputable "skid row" bars.

A notorious part of that cluster on South Front Street, the Portside Lounge, had recently closed. "Everything that can be done will be done to keep a license from being issued to reopen a similar establishment," the committee's minutes stated. The bar was owned by a guy named Buddy Best. He also owned another bar on "skid row," the Barbary Coast at 115 S. Front St. I was asked to explore buying the Portside Lounge building—without using DARE's name. I had already met with Best, who asked $125,000 for a property that wasn't worth more than $40,000. Committee members suggested hiring me as DARE's real estate agent so I could put down $1,000 on a purchase option for the property. That would keep someone from opening another bar there "and to give time to arrange a way to gain full control of the building."

I accepted that challenge. On Aug. 9, 1985, in a memo to Murphrey, I proposed a land swap, using that $1,000 from DARE. That deal would depend on the condition "that Buddy Best must relocate his Barbary Coast Bar business to the new location, or at least out of its present location on South Front Street." As it turned out, we never did oust the Barbary Coast. That establishment, the last of the "skid row" bars, remains open to this day, but it's now a popular throwback with an edgy, vintage "dive bar" vibe, attracting a far different clientele than it and its neighbors had once served.

In response to a DARE effort to improve the standards of downtown's bars, the Barbary Coast had a sign made. Years later, it still cheekily declares, "We're upped our standards. Up yours!" I can't argue with a pitch-perfect sentiment like that.

During the next couple of decades, while busy with my own projects and a few other causes, I remained close to DARE. In 2001, Bob Murphrey resigned from DARE after seventeen years in the top job. I was called back to serve as interim executive director. That temporary gig ended when Susi Hamilton, then a city planner, took the permanent job.

* * *

I should mention a few other efforts that began during my time at DARE, but didn't get resolved until later years.

One of those was the most prominent of the ugly false fronts that had disfigured downtown buildings since the 1950s. Both faces of the Solomon building at Front and Market were covered by a semi-transparent screen of rigid metal panels. During the years that DARE had been lending money to remove such façades elsewhere, this building's owner, Harold Greene, had resisted.

In late 1984, Bob Murphrey had obtained bids from contractors, which he passed on to the owner. He shared historical research about the building's origins in the 1890s and its "historical, architectural and cultural significance." None of that moved the needle.

As DARE's executive director in the late 20th Century, Bob Murphrey completed several major projects that the author had begun.

But eventually, three years later, Greene finally accepted that stripping off the metal panels wasn't just good for downtown's image; it would benefit him by improving the value of his property.

Here's how Murphrey explained it in a September 1987 memo: "This building has long been a highly visible eyesore and many efforts have been made to encourage its rehabilitation. This attempt has been successful due to DARE and city efforts to secure a tenant for the vacant upper floors, and below-rate financing." That tenant was to be the non-profit Legal Services agency, whose budget didn't permit it to pay market rental rates.

I got involved in my role as a real estate appraiser. That same month, I informed Greene that "after renovation" his building would be worth $315,000—equivalent to $885,000 today. Finally sweetening the pot was a $20,000 DARE façade-rehab loan, the latest of its kind from the revolving loan fund we had established almost a decade earlier.

The building, with its elegant Nineteenth-Century brickwork and window treatments, is now a beautiful part of the downtown streetscape. It currently houses the Seabird Restaurant.

* * *

In 1987, on the tenth anniversary of DARE's incorporation, the *Sunday Star-News* devoted a full page to a look back on what we had accomplished. Some statistics helped tell the story. In ten years, downtown's tax base had almost tripled, from $34 million in 1977 to more than $91 million a decade later. Investments in that time included construction or rehabilitation of

150 downtown buildings. Employment had also grown, despite the loss of merchants to the mall: In 1976, 4,781 people worked in the Central Business District. In 1986, that number was 6,032.

And despite the traumatic transition from mass merchandising to specialty and tourist-oriented shops, even retail sales had risen, from less than $31 million to over $47 million.

The story included this observation: "Revitalizing downtown remains a struggle but nowhere near the obstacle that confronted Merritt and Mary Gornto." It also quoted Bob Murphrey, who was running DARE at the time, about what we had been up against: "They had nothing to sell in the early days except for blind faith. From 1976 to 1980, things were really on the skids." A newspaper editorial marking the anniversary added this: "Thanks to enthusiasm and faith, dollars and deals, gambles and guts, downtown has regained its historic role as the place that defines Wilmington. Setbacks continue, of course, but hammers and paint brushes still fly, and a new hotel and conference center are about to rise on the river. Few cities have done better."

That remains true today. As recently as January 2025, the *StarNews* was reporting that downtown's retail space was ninety-eight percent occupied! For office space, the occupancy rate was ninety-five percent. The Central Business District had taxable property valued at $760 million, a major asset for both city and county governments.

2. Liquor by the Drink

North Carolina has always had a love-hate relationship with alcohol. Our state enacted Prohibition in 1909, a decade before the rest of the nation did. Vestiges of Prohibition remained in effect here for decades after it had ended everywhere else. That meant that as late as the 1970s, it was illegal for North Carolina's restaurants or bars to serve hard liquor of any kind.

If you wanted to sip on, say, a gin and tonic with your dinner, you'd first have to make a stop at your nearest Alcoholic Beverage Control store and buy yourself a whole bottle of gin. Then, assuming the restaurant had the right kind of license, you'd carry your bottle to your table, camouflaged in a brown paper bag. Your waiter would bring you a glass, the tonic, some ice, and a slice of lime—sold as a "set-up"—and you would pour your own liquor. As much as you wanted. And as often as you wanted, too, limited only by the need to keep buying fresh set-ups. Unless, as sometimes happened, you were willing to sneak some booze right out of your bottle.

It won't surprise anyone to know that this awkward arrangement didn't suit either restaurants or their customers very well. Imagine a first-time vacationer from most any other state, accustomed to routinely ordering a cocktail with their meal, discovering that it wasn't possible here. Our state's outdated liquor laws were a serious drag on tourism. They also weren't helping things downtown, where DARE, Inc. was having little success in recruiting new restaurants.

By the mid-1970s, things were coming to a head. The state's hospitality industry—not just restaurants and hotels, but also other businesses that depended on tourist traffic—began agitating to bring the state's liquor laws up to date. Or, at the very least, to allow for sale of liquor by the drink.

It was a Wilmington legislator, State Sen. William G. Smith, who pushed the liquor-by-the-drink bill through both Senate and House of Representatives in June 1977. It was a closely fought campaign. It passed the state Senate by only a couple of votes; was sent back and forth between the full House of Representatives and its alcohol-control committee; and finally stayed alive, on a second reading, by a single vote. But by the third and final reading, Smith's bill got House approval by a 62-55 vote. It became law on July 1, 1977.

The simple phrase "liquor by the drink," by the way, would be shortened to "LBD" in headlines and other media references, right up there with "ABC." Those initials stand for "Alcoholic Beverage Control," which is what North Carolina still calls its patchwork system of county or city-operated liquor stores.

After Bill Smith got his bill passed, the next step was up to our Board of County Commissioners. On June 19, 1978, the commissioners voted three to two to put the matter before the voters. The holdouts were Claud "Buck" O'Shields and Vivian Wright. Those favoring the people's right to vote on this question were Karen Gottovi, Ellen Williams, and George Alper. And while the actual date would be up to the Board of Elections, limited by law to either forty-five days before or forty-five days after the November general election, the commissioners' majority recommended a January referendum. That would give New Hanover County voters a chance to see what their counterparts in other resort communities decided, and to consider the potential economic benefits from increased tourism. As it happened, several nearby towns in Brunswick County would hold LBD referendums in September 1978, providing a useful precedent for supporters here to build on.

We were pleased when every one of them passed. Leading the way were Southport, Sunset Beach, Calabash, and the two towns (Long Beach and Yaupon Beach) that are now the consolidated municipality of Oak Island.

Here in New Hanover County, the two commissioners who voted "No" insisted that no referendum should be called unless LBD supporters could collect signatures on a petition to force one. Their argument ended up going nowhere. It certainly didn't help the foot-draggers' cause when the business community, as represented by the Chamber of Commerce, endorsed the referendum. H. Van Reid, the Chamber's top administrator, urged the commissioners to "take a leadership role."

Organizing a Coalition

How the pro-LBD forces got organized contains several lessons for Citizen Warriors.

My day job with DARE made it impractical for me to hold a formal leadership position. We would need a committee. Eventually, this movement would coalesce into the Committee for a Better Way, though it was sometimes also called the New Hanover County Mixed Beverage Committee.

It originated in several places, from a diverse mix of people, coming together to work for a common cause. All three of its co-chairs had experience in political activism, and each had ties to important constituencies among potential voters.

One who stepped up to help was a long-time activist, Kay Sebian. First in New Jersey and then in North Carolina, she and her husband Al were long-time fixtures in Democratic Party politics. Her other causes included Planned Parenthood, the League of Women Voters, and the effort to get the Equal Rights Amendment ratified by our state legislature. For a time, she worked in the City of Wilmington's Human Relations office.

The second co-chair was an ambitious young man, originally from Gary, Indiana, who worked at Sears, Roebuck. His name was Tony Pate. He'd always been interested in public affairs, so much so that he had filed as a candidate for a Wilmington City Council seat in 1977, when he was just twenty-six years old. By his own admission years later, he didn't know what he was doing. And so he had dropped out of that election before the ballots were printed.

But he never dropped his political ambitions, which would get him elected to the Council just two years later. In the meantime, to get himself better prepared, he became a Democratic Party precinct chairman. He helped Democratic candidates in the 1978 elections, including my father, who won his State House seat that year. Among his political mentors was a doctor, Dan Gottovi, husband of County Commissioner Karen Gottovi. Those connections helped get Pate involved in the liquor-by-the-drink effort.

It was through our work on Karen Gottovi's 1976 election campaign, as well as that of the late City Councilman Rupert Bryan in 1977, that I got to know the third co-chair, Camilla Bain. Besides her political work, Cammy Bain had worked as a reporter at the *Morning Star*. She was well-connected in what we might call the city's do-gooder community. She also had impeccable establishment credentials; her husband was a partner in one of Wilmington's leading law firms.

In some of those political-insider conversations, the matter of liquor by the drink had come up. The Democratic Party activists soon found themselves "in a room with people we didn't know," as Pate put it: The restaurateurs and hotel owners for whom the matter of brown-bagging versus mixed drinks directly affected their livelihoods.

* * *

My public role was to be the group's spokesman to the news media. And although eventually I had to give up that position, I still did all I could behind the scenes.

Meanwhile, Cammy Bain took over much of the media work. "Our job involved being on television quite frequently," she recalled recently. Even on the night of the election, she said, before celebrating our victory, "I had to rush downtown to go on television."

"We really hit it off," was how Pate characterized our committee's working relationship. We put together a plan. Besides the media contacts, it included holding events to motivate potential voters and organizing a speaker's bureau to deliver our message to civic groups. We also focused on recruiting volunteers to contact voters individually, as well as getting hotels that supported the cause to donate rooms to be used as phone banks. Before they could begin making phone calls, though, the volunteers needed names and numbers.

That's where my father's political connections came in handy. During that year's successful campaign for the State House, he had obtained invaluable voter-registration data. He shared those precinct lists, derived from public records, with our liquor-by-the-drink campaign. Because voter-registration data doesn't include phone numbers, it took "just a little bit of work to look up the phone numbers," as Bain said. In those days, of course, just about everybody in town was listed in the Southern Bell phone book. And so we organized several dozen volunteers, usually six to ten at a time in a hotel office, to devote a couple of hours each evening making phone calls. It was a disciplined effort. The volunteers were trained, as Pate explained, to quickly make their case, avoid arguing, "to follow the script, say 'Thank you,' and hang up."

* * *

Obviously, this campaign was very important to my job with DARE. Improving the profitability of downtown's restaurants and hotels, not to mention creating conditions that would lure new players into those fields, was a top priority for our group. It was also important for other business organizations such as the Chamber of Commerce. The LBD campaign truly transcended party lines. The coalition that formed around it put liberal Democrats to work side by side with conservative Republican businessmen for the whole community's benefit.

However, my employment by an organization largely funded by city and county governments created some issues. The November 1978 minutes of the DARE Executive Committee explain: "Merritt had been working on the New Hanover Committee for a Better Way, promoting a mixed beverage referendum yes vote for Jan. 12, 1979 and . . . had been asked to be the spokesman for the group." I asked the committee for its opinion. The conclusion: They considered this a conflict of interest. So I agreed to resign as the LBD group's spokesman. (Not that I stopped working on its behalf.)

Minutes later, I was pleased that DARE's Executive Committee immediately recommended that our full Board of Directors endorse the mixed beverage initiative.

One discreet way I was able to help was to let the Committee for a Better Way use space in the vacant Trust Building at Front and Market streets. As DARE executive, I had been tasked with finding tenants for that tall, narrow office building. I had a lot of flexibility in that role, which extended to supplying the committee with keys to the building.

Kay Sebian Cammy Bain Tony Pate
Co-chairs of The Committee for a Better Way

The committee's routine, Pate explained, was to meet there every Sunday over coffee and plan which hotel the phone bank would be using the following week. The committee also made decisions about how to use donated money. One tactic was to produce a TV spot, in the process learning how commercials were scripted, filmed and edited. "That was really fun," Pate remembered.

To help with the technicalities of public outreach, we hired a graphics firm. They produced our campaign's highest-profile element: A large poster. This was widely distributed around town, prominently displayed in restaurants, bars, and other public spaces. It featured a vintage engraving of a Victorian gentleman in a top hat, obviously drunk, leaning against a wall and clutching a bottle. The headline read, "I only wanted one drink, but I had to buy a bottle." That summed up our campaign's main argument, one that helped undercut the opponents' anti-alcohol preaching: That the brown-bag status quo was a far stronger contributor to alcohol abuse than the regulated sale of cocktails would be. "There's a better way," Pate recalled, and that phrase was central to our campaign.

Reaching and Registering Young Voters

Because of my job with DARE, I couldn't be one of the campaign's official leaders. But Pate would say about me much later, "He was always around. He was always trying to do stuff for downtown." That doesn't sound very sophisticated. But it does nicely sum up one of the principles of effective citizen leadership: Be there, show up, be available. And be ready to work.

Of course, we weren't the only ones focused on the referendum. Our opponents got organized, too. In late September 1978, about fifty people met to set up the New Hanover County Christian Action League, and elect the Rev. Horace Jackson as its president. Jackson, who was pastor of Sunset Park Baptist Church, called on his anti-liquor allies to "prepare ourselves for battle." In comments about how his opponents might push our cause, Rev. Jackson let us know what he thought of us. "This is the devil's way of doing business," he declared.

Although the question on the ballot would be simply about how, not whether, liquor should be sold, Jackson took an absolutist position. He urged his followers to oppose the sale of liquor "in its every form."

We agreed with him, up to a point: We wanted to end the sale of liquor by the bottle to be carried into restaurants. And it's likely that our more nuanced position, which both drinkers and non-drinkers could support, made a big difference in the eventual result.

The "anti" forces took great comfort from the results of a failed 1973 state-wide referendum on liquor by the drink. On the other hand, we in the

This poster made the essential point that the old 'brown-bag' system encouraged alcohol abuse. That message to voters was a potent counter to the 'anti' mixed-beverage forces, the most vocal of whom made an absolutist argument against any sale or consumption of alcohol. Helping the 'pro' side in the 1979 referendum were younger voters, new arrivals in town, and New Hanover County's hotel and restaurant businesses.

"pro" camp remembered that in New Hanover County, that 1973 measure had been defeated by a razor-thin margin of only 130 votes.

It's noteworthy that our own county ABC Board and its top officials all predicted that voters would reject LBD. One ABC Board member, W. Eugene Edwards, declared in August 1978 that the issue couldn't pass with the restrictions the law imposed. The board's lawyer, Cicero Yow, agreed. "Those amendments were put on to kill it," he asserted. And the local ABC administrator, W. Douglas Powell, piled on too. They all insisted that the special tax on booze sold to restaurants would be unenforceable, that extra law enforcement would be needed, and that police would need "accounting backgrounds" to be able to examine restaurants' business records.

Of course, they were wrong. Not just about what voters would decide, but also about how the LBD regulations supposedly couldn't be enforced. For the past forty-six years, as it turned out, the ABC authorities have been managing their oversight responsibilities pretty well.

One of our strategies was to encourage new voter registrations by people who lived in apartment complexes. Those tended to be fairly recent arrivals in town, younger, or both. We scheduled a series of wine-and-cheese parties at seven different rental-housing sites. We also sponsored a barbecue at the Sportsmen's Club on Castle Street and a rally at the Martin Luther King Center on South Eighth Street to appeal to Black voters. And while the county Board of Elections declined our invitation to send registrars to these events and sign up prospective voters, it did agree to open its main registration office on the three Saturday mornings before the referendum.

"We think our support is going to come from young people," Bain was quoted in a newspaper report during the lead-up to the vote. We based our approach on what had helped get an earlier Mecklenburg County referendum passed. There, in Charlotte and its suburbs, the county Board of Elections had sent registrars to the pro-LBD apartment parties to sign up new voters. (Also in Charlotte: After their referendum, North Carolina's first legal cocktail—a bloody Mary—would be poured there on Nov. 21, 1978.)

Bain's opinion about youthful voters was influenced by some personal encounters with older voters who liked brown-bagging and wanted to keep it. That was another "anti" demographic we had to contend with. Bain remembered a confrontation with her husband's law partner, the late John J. Burney, Jr. He was a powerful man, a former state senator, with plenty of political clout of his own. "He raked me over the coals" about her involvement with the LBD campaign, she remembered, "because this would make liquor too expensive."

Incidents like that helped reassure us that we were correct to focus on younger voters. Our voter-registration effort clearly paid off. New Hanover County reported more than 500 new registrations between the November 1978 general election and the January 1979 liquor referendum.

As with so many of the causes I have espoused, this one benefitted from media attention and support. On Nov. 22, 1978, the *Morning Star* endorsed a "yes" vote with an editorial under the headline "Liquor by drink should be passed in New Hanover." The editorial stated, "The issue is not one of morality," noting that the state had addressed that forty years earlier. That was when North Carolina set up its ABC system after national prohibition was repealed. The decision, the endorsement went on, was "Whether we continue to sell it by the bottle—up to a gallon at a time—or by the drink; whether individuals can walk into a restaurant and straight-forwardly order up a drink, or whether that individual should tote it in by the bag, almost surreptitiously, and pour it." The editorial went on to itemize the many things "southeastern North Carolina has going for it," including the pending construction of I-40, pending opening of Independence Mall, and "the steady regeneration and interest in downtown Wilmington." The conclusion: "It is all positive, and liquor by the drink is a realistic complement to the growing importance of the area."

Despite that editorial-page support, the newspaper's news columns gave plenty of coverage to Rev. Jackson and other LBD opponents. Even so, one disgruntled person at the Christian Action League's September meeting insisted that the *Morning Star* was "not going to give us one ounce, one inch of coverage."

The weekend before the referendum, the *Morning Star* published a feature that addressed all the strange quirks in state liquor laws around the country. Those absurdities included the rules in South Carolina, Alabama, and Utah that required that all mixed drinks sold in restaurants be poured from mini-bottles—a provision that Sen. Bill Smith and his legislative allies had swatted away when his bill was being debated in the General Assembly.

State Senator William G. Smith of Wilmington

Two days later, WWAY-TV3 hosted a televised debate between Senator Smith and Rev. Jackson. In front of a live audience, it featured questions from three journalists: John Randt and Stella Shelton of Channel 3 and Bob Hill of the *Morning Star*.

The Committee for a Better Way decided against participating. "We didn't think it would be productive," Tony Pate recalled. We didn't see any benefit in confronting a potentially hostile audience. As he explained our position: "We were the good guys" who didn't have to prove ourselves.

Senator Smith had no such qualms. He proved a worthy spokesman for the cause, both on TV and, a day later, in a transcript that the *Morning Star* printed in full.

Wilmington Morning Star
LBD passes nearly 2-1

The 'Morning Star' headline left no doubt about the referendum's overwhelming result.

"It seems to me," Smith said in his opening statement, "that people will drink less when they're paying $1.85 to $2 a drink than they will when they're buying it by the fifth or quart, at $5 or $6 a bottle." He then addressed the potential economic impact, and referred to what had happened when Richmond, Va. took a similar step. "In Richmond, I'm told that within thirty days after the mixed beverage option was selected there, the building department had applications for over $30 million worth of new construction of restaurants alone. It's estimated that there are about 265 restaurants, hotels and motels in New Hanover County, which would be eligible for a mixed beverage license if the referendum passes." Based on surveys he had seen, Smith predicted that a "yes" vote for LBD would stimulate "the construction of perhaps ten new restaurants" and two new hotels valued "somewhere in the neighborhood of $15 million."

Rev. Jackson replied by complaining that "we have seen our liquor laws liberalized continually to the point that this ABC is coming to mean 'Absolutely Beyond Control.'" He pooh-poohed the argument that liquor by the drink would enhance either tourism or the convention trade. Jackson went on to argue that LBD would increase alcohol consumption, drunk-driving accidents and arrests, and fatalities. "We cannot afford to take the risk that is before us."

Smith responded by questioning statistics Jackson had cited concerning alcohol-related problems in Virginia and South Carolina. He pointed out that on a per-capita basis, drunk-driving arrests had declined in both neighboring states. He also said that while he didn't know whether LBD would increase tourism here, Raleigh and Wake County had seen "plans to build a multi-million-dollar hotel to support the convention center there," which depended entirely on approval of mixed-drink sales.

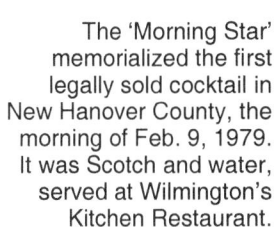

The 'Morning Star' memorialized the first legally sold cocktail in New Hanover County, the morning of Feb. 9, 1979. It was Scotch and water, served at Wilmington's Kitchen Restaurant.

An Electoral Triumph Brings Economic Blessings

Finally, decision time arrived. Jan. 12, 1979 was an unusual Friday election day. The referendum was held on a cold, rainy winter day, but despite our fears that this might erode our support, participation was robust. All told, 18,790 people cast ballots, a remarkable 43 percent turnout for a special election.

Awaiting the results after the polls closed, we got highly encouraging news when the first precinct reported. As it happened, that was the Sunset Park neighborhood, home of Rev. Jackson's Sunset Park Baptist Church. Because Sunset Park was considered a "dry" stronghold, we interpreted that precinct's narrow 325-264 "no" vote as a sign of the "anti" camp's weakness. As the rest of the county's results poured in, they confirmed that judgment. The result was a nearly two-to-one victory, 11,849 for mixed drinks and only 6,941 against. Only four of the county's thirty-four precincts returned a "no" majority. Overwhelmingly, New Hanover's voters agreed with us.

Immediately after that vote, both government and business leaders were predicting significant economic growth as a result.

The first legal "mixed drinks" to be sold here in nearly seventy years were poured on the morning of Feb. 9, 1979. The very first of those, a Scotch and water, was sold to one Jesse M. Hale at the bar of the former Kitchen restaurant on Carolina Beach Road. He took that first legal sip at

9:57 a.m. The next day's *Morning Star* reported that he had become "a footnote in local history." The Kitchen was one of twenty restaurants that sold mixed drinks that first day.

The number of mixed-drink establishments tripled in just a month. The *Sunday Star-News* annual "Progress" supplement, published Feb. 25, predicted that still more would get licensed in time for the summer tourist season, and quoted local officials saying this would spur construction of major new hotels and restaurants. The newspaper reported that $2 million worth of expansions, renovations and new construction of hotels and restaurants were already under way or being planned.

A big chunk of that investment came from one of the referendum's active supporters. The Hilton Inn downtown (now doing business under Hilton's "Ballast" brand) had been DARE's biggest original private-sector funder. But because it had to make major investments in upgrading its restaurant and lounge before beginning mixed-drink sales, the Hilton wouldn't begin offering cocktails until several months after its competitors did. Soon, it would have many more of those competitors.

Shortly after the vote, Joe Augustine, who had replaced Van Reid as the Chamber of Commerce's top executive, told the *Morning Star* that two national firms had already taken options on land for hotels to be valued around $10 million each. He and other business leaders tied legal liquor sales to important infrastructure projects, notably expansion of the port and new four-lane highways. Put together, it all "virtually assures new investments and employment opportunities," the paper declared.

Senator Smith predicted, "I'm convinced that New Hanover County and southeastern North Carolina are going to experience the greatest economic prosperity over the next ten to fifteen years that they've ever even dreamed of."

Less than three weeks in, the *Morning Star* did a follow-up report. They interviewed me, among other sources. The consensus: Business was brisk and problems were few. "It came in without a lot of hoopla," the article quoted me. "The transition was very smooth," and had already helped to stabilize several new downtown restaurants. LBD was crucial, I said: "They need it to survive."

One downtown restaurant owner, Jerry Piner of Three Penny Gallery in The Cotton Exchange, said he was already seeing customers eating out more often and spending more. That extra spending, he and others agreed, was mostly for sophisticated cocktails. At Wrightsville Beach, Burks Hamner of the Blockade Runner hotel was quoted saying, "We're getting a lot of people out that we haven't seen before."

Another Wrightsville Beach restaurateur, Michael Newton of the old Apple Annie's Restaurant, predicted that the new mixed-drink regime would help our tourism community outdraw the competition in Myrtle Beach, S.C. Because liquor by the drink on the other side of the state line relied on mini-bottles, like you'd buy on an airplane, ordering a cocktail was both inconvenient and costly compared to having it mixed by a bartender. With new, improved rules here, Newton said, "I think it's a great boost for the beach itself."

Within two months, thirty-four New Hanover County establishments had obtained mixed-drink permits. Under the state law as it stood at the time, these had to be either restaurants—required to prove they earned at least half their income from selling food—or private clubs. The law's private-club provision meant that many a bar that couldn't qualify as a restaurant began selling "memberships" for as little as a dollar. But over the years, the state relaxed those rules to the point that buying a cocktail here is now essentially the same as in most other states. But even as awkward as the initial LBD rules were, they were far less awkward than the old brown-bag system.

By that time, the end of April 1979, the old brown-bag permits had expired. That affected about ninety businesses countywide.

A year after mixed-drink sales began, Wilmington Police reported that drunken-driving arrests had declined by about five percent since the end of brown-bagging. That was a welcome confirmation of our argument that letting bartenders, not customers themselves, control drinkers' consumption would reduce alcohol abuse. What was then known as the Southeastern Mental Health Center had similar findings. Its caseload related to alcohol abuse had stabilized, if not actually decreased, Tony Nichols of SEMH said in April 1980. "People are not drinking as heavily," he said. "They go into a bar, have a couple of drinks and then leave."

New Hanover County's ABC system reported that liquor consumption remained stable during the first year of liquor by the drink, contrasted with a nine-percent increase in alcohol sales statewide. That may have been related to the fact that ninety-nine of the state's ABC jurisdictions had not considered LBD and that nine had rejected mixed-drink sales. New

Hanover was among only twenty-eight ABC systems—they included all of the biggest cities and urban counties—that had approved liquor by the drink.

* * *

One narrow measure of economic impact is the number of restaurants now, compared to the bad old days of brown-bagging. Looking just at downtown Wilmington, the Central Business District had just fourteen restaurants, according to the 1978 *Hill's City Directory*. Also, nine bars were operating, including two topless joints and a half-dozen dives along the South Front Street "skid row," serving nothing stronger than beer and wine.

In 2024, by contrast, according to the *Polk City Directory*, the Central Business District was home to more than forty restaurants and fourteen bars. The New Hanover County ABC system reported that, as of early 2025, 450 establishments countywide held mixed-beverage licenses.

State-wide, liquor sales generate more than $1 billion in revenue annually, with nearly half of that going to the state's General Fund and to the local governments that run the ABC stores. Of that more than $430 million, the ABC Commission says, the state got about $323 million and localities collected the rest.

But those numbers don't address the indirect benefits from profitable restaurants, from tourism, and from development that's steered toward communities that allow liquor by the drink. In 2015, UNC-Charlotte's Urban Institute published a commentary about the economic benefits that mixed-drink sales bring to local communities. "Planners and others say alcohol sales are a primary catalyst for attracting restaurants and stores, many of which depend heavily on alcohol sales to make a profit," the piece said.

It quoted Mike Herring, who had recently retired as administrator of the state ABC Commission. During his thirty-three years with the agency, he watched as liquor by the drink was approved by one county or town after another, and he saw how it attracted major investments. For example, Herring said, "If Charlotte didn't have liquor-by-the-drink, they wouldn't have the Carolina Panthers and all the professional sports."

* * *

Essential as it was, getting liquor-by-the-drink approved wasn't the end of the story. North Carolina's peculiar, patchwork ABC system was still full of odd contradictions and strange obstacles for business. Decades later, I thought it was important enough to do something about it. In 2014, I incorporated the non-profit North Carolinians for ABC Reform.

Neither time nor space permit me to get into the many issues that afflicted the state's byzantine ABC system at the time. Suffice it to say that I had no trouble finding allies among the many people and businesses frustrated by the mess.

In 2019, a legislative study commission recommended a series of reforms. These were meant to improve the profitability of local ABC systems and eliminate rules that unnecessarily burdened restaurants and other establishments.

Finally, in 2024, the General Assembly enacted an "ABC Omnibus Bill" that modernized many aspects of the state's alcohol control system. It didn't accomplish everything the 2019 report called for, but it was a significant improvement. And of course it built on the progress so many of us made back in the 1970s.

So next time you're out to dinner or enjoying a night on the town, pause over that cocktail and raise a toast to the long-ago Citizen Warriors—and the voters—who made it all possible.

In the effort to block a coal-exporting terminal from the downtown waterfront, the author (left) enlisted the help of his father, Eugene W. Merritt, Sr., seen here in the late 1970s examining renovation work on Princess Street, a few doors from the DARE, Inc. office.

3. Wilmington Versus the Coal Pile

The most critical and challenging struggle I faced in promoting downtown Wilmington's redevelopment was the fight to prevent a coal-exporting terminal from being built right on the waterfront. Looking back, it seems incredible that most of Wilmington's powers that be were comfortable with the prospect of a huge mountain of coal looming over downtown. That would have been right where the Wilmington Convention Center and the Embassy Suites hotel now stand. But it's true: We faced an uphill fight to stop a project that would have permanently blighted our city.

By 1981, when this story began, the greater Wilmington region had become a target for a long list of companies that hoped to take advantage of cheap land, high unemployment, and local governments eager for boosts to their tax base.

Throughout the 1980s, even into the mid-1990s, a series of potentially disastrous industrial-development proposals threatened our region's largely pristine environment. First of these came from a consortium of oil companies that planned to build a major refinery on the Brunswick County bank of the Cape Fear River, just a few miles downstream from downtown Wilmington. That project, estimated to cost between $350 and $450 million, was to have begun operating in 1983, producing 100,000 to 150,000 barrels of gasoline a day. With a promised property tax bill of about $1.2 million, it immediately got endorsements from Brunswick County politicians. But both state and federal officials were more cautious, warning of possible environmental problems.

That project, under the name Brunswick Energy Company, was still pending in early 1981, but environmental groups were pushing back, hard.

It wasn't the only major environmental threat. In 1980 and 1981, a major aluminum smelter was being proposed for Columbus County, again just a few miles outside of Wilmington. And again, two groups were up in arms: Neighbors concerned about negative effects on their property as well as environmentalists worried about pollution and destruction of natural habitats.

For downtown Wilmington, the most serious of these threats concerned coal.

That materialized in early 1981, during my third year as executive director of DARE, Inc. It was an exciting time for downtown, but also a perilous one. Both the city government and private interests were making major investments in infrastructure and new businesses. But the progress we had started making might easily have been undone.

As an old seaport, Wilmington had always had an industrial waterfront right next to its downtown business district. In the 1980s, just a stone's throw from The Cotton Exchange and what was then called Cape Fear Technical Institute, that included remnants of the old Atlantic Coast Line Railroad. The ACL, a parent company of today's CSX, had its headquarters in Wilmington until 1960. Two decades later, what remained along the Cape Fear River included some unused railroad tracks, a diesel-fuel tank farm, and several old warehouses. Between that site and the Northeast Cape Fear River Bridge was nothing but a complex of bulk-cargo warehouses, many of them deteriorating and abandoned.

While those decaying industrial properties were mostly lying fallow, something important was happening in international trade. America's coal mines were producing more than domestic users needed, at the same time that spiking oil prices had raised demand for alternative fuels in Europe. Demand there was outstripping domestic coal supplies. And so the coal-export business was booming. Old, established shipping terminals, like CSX Railroad's massive facility in Newport News, Va., were running full tilt and still facing backlogs of thirty to sixty days. That encouraged new entrants to try their hands at the coal-export business.

Those included my former employer, North Carolina's State Ports Authority, which hoped to jump on that bandwagon. In its plans for 1981, the SPA proposed developing a coal-export facility at the state-owned terminal south of downtown. To be leased to a Kentucky company called Carol Coal Co., it would have required at least three trains a day, carrying up to six million tons of coal a year, to pass through several Wilmington neighborhoods on their way to the port. Several other companies were looking at the Cape Fear River, including Kentucky-based Cleancoal Terminals, American Coal Export Co. of Edenton, N.C., the General Electric subsidiary Utah International Corp., and Williams Terminals Co.

In February 1981, American Coal Export announced plans for an 85-acre site on the Northeast Cape Fear River. That plan, at least, had the benefit of keeping coal trains out of the city. But a year later, that company hadn't lined up firm contracts with shippers or acquired needed permits. Utah International had secured an option on a site on the Brunswick County side of the Cape Fear River and was proposing to handle five million tons of coal a year. But by late 1981, it let its option lapse, citing a decline in European demand for coal. Around the same time, though, the Williams company entered the competition with plans for a ten-million-ton export terminal near the river's mouth, just north of Southport.

It wasn't just that coal exports would be dirty and a blight on their neighbors. At least one of them would have also cost the City of Wilmington millions just to protect its water supply. The American Coal Export project would have required deepening the Northeast Cape Fear River's shipping channel from twenty-two feet to thirty-five. And that would have required that the city's two large water-supply pipes, which run under the river, be lowered by ten feet. To meet the estimated $1.5 million cost of that work, the city proposed applying for an Urban Development Action Grant. UDAG was the same federal program, meant to encourage investment in "distressed" cities, that we were using to get the Riverwalk started downtown. In this case, the UDAG money would have been a federal subsidy to a private industry, combined with the company's own money to dredge the channel and build coal-loading wharves.

The most worrisome of these was the proposal from Cleancoal. Then as now, of course, the name was a contradiction in terms. There is no such thing as "clean" coal. But the real contradiction would come between that company's ambitions and our city's future. Looking for a seaport with good

Piles of coal up to four stories high, railroad tracks, and ship-loading machinery much like this might easily have dominated the northern part of Wilmington's downtown waterfront.

rail connections to the coalfields, as well as plenty of cheap available land, its investors had discovered Wilmington. And in Wilmington, they found, the old ACL tract was idle, available for purchase, and already zoned for the sort of industries that once operated there. Cleancoal formed a North Carolina corporation called Wilmington Coal Transfer, Inc., to develop its project.

A Looming Threat to Downtown

But already by 1980, downtown Wilmington's industrial past had given way to a new vision of the riverfront as an amenity for hospitality, for waterfront dining, for hotels with a river view, and as a site for an urgently needed convention center. As described in the previous chapter, groups including the Chamber of Commerce had been trying to rally support for a publicly funded venue for large meetings and events, and the most obvious location was downtown. But now, suddenly, a polluting industry, dirtier and uglier than anything we had seen before, was threatening to encroach on downtown. This came at downtown's most vulnerable moment: Right after the final departure of retailers to Independence Mall, just as the first major revitalization projects were tentatively getting off the ground.

It should have been obvious that a coal-exporting terminal on the river was a direct threat to all our work downtown. But some important people didn't see it that way.

Instead, after voters said 'no' to the coal-exporting terminal, the site where the coal pile would have loomed is now home to the Wilmington Convention Center and adjacent hotel.

Politically speaking, there were strong voices on the Wilmington City Council favoring the coal project. They thought this would be "good business." They argued that the coal operation could be accommodated as long as "safety precautions" were maintained. This attitude greatly worried me, as well as many other people who shared my vision for a new, non-industrial downtown. Fortunately, that meant I had plenty of support for my opposition to the coal project. But what could be done? Especially considering the project's support from influential politicians.

The situation called for leadership. In part because of my position as the public voice of downtown Wilmington's revitalization effort, I felt that I needed to be that leader: Someone to manage the struggle to stop Cleancoal. But I also concluded that I needed to keep a low profile, working mostly behind the scenes. Because the DARE board included some members who favored the coal pile, I needed to remain discreet in public.

And so I recruited a valuable ally, who could be our cause's public face: My father. By now, he was out of the state legislature, but he hadn't lost his focus on the public interest. What might have been one of his greatest contributions to this fight was to reframe the terms of the debate.

Instead of the mealy-mouthed "export terminal," he routinely used the blunt—and accurate—phrase "coal pile" to make it clear to everybody just what we were facing. He got plenty of media attention, raising public awareness of what was at stake, while I was struggling behind the scenes to find a winning strategy.

Of course, it wouldn't be just the "pile." A huge apparatus of clanking, banging machinery would also be needed. Getting coal out of railroad hopper cars would require massive dumping equipment, conveyor belts, and the like. Even with water-spraying measures to minimize the amount of airborne coal dust that would have drifted away into the rest of downtown, the site would have been dirty, with every surface and the ground itself tainted with a wet, coal-dust sludge, laden with toxic heavy metals.

Then there would be the trains. As you'll see in a later chapter, I am a big believer in passenger railroads, a service I enjoyed in my youth and that I'm working today to restore to Wilmington. But a shiny string of Amtrak coaches is a far cry from a mile-long train of coal hoppers, which should have no place in any city's commercial center.

* * *

By the summer of 1981, the proposal had attracted both high-level support and widespread opposition.

To shore up support for its plans, Cleancoal put on a lobbying blitz. In June, it flew fifteen Wilmington leaders, including Mayor Halterman and Joe Augustine, president of the Chamber of Commerce, to tour its facilities in Kentucky.

The opposition, I'm happy to say, started with DARE, Inc. In June, I gave a report on the coal pile to DARE's Executive Committee. I mentioned that, along with Rick Willetts, I would be visiting the nearest coal-shipping facility, at the Morehead City port. For the moment, the committee decided to postpone any action until we had studied the matter further.

After making that information-gathering trip to Morehead City, I got back to the full DARE Board. On July 29, 1981, I recommended a resolution opposing Cleancoal's plans. I said the coal pile would have "a detrimental effect on the image of downtown as a tourist destination and as a city supposedly dedicated to the revitalization of its waterfront." It would devalue nearby property. Large investments, both public and private, in Cape Fear Technical Institute, The Cotton Exchange, and elsewhere in the Central Business District "will be in trouble," I warned.

Directly addressing one of our opponents' arguments, I pointed out that the coal pile would add little to the property tax base. Acre for acre, industrial land has a low tax value; "The appropriate use for the property is commercial.... The continuation of low-density, low tax value development will place negative downward pressure on urban land values."

Then I itemized the inevitable environmental damage from both air and water pollution.

Finally, I told the DARE board that putting a coal pile on the downtown waterfront would conflict with the city's policies in favor of downtown revitalization, of historic preservation, and of redeveloping the waterfront to encourage commerce and tourism.

On Aug. 13, the board approved a resolution that reiterated my arguments. It said the coal pile "will give the surrounding area an industrial flavor not compatible with the preservation efforts currently under way in downtown Wilmington and contributing to its uniqueness."

The Board did hedge on one point. "While we support Wilmington Cleancoal Transfer, Inc.'s proposed operation in Wilmington," the resolution said, "we are of the opinion that the proposed site adjacent to the Central Business District will be a detriment to the future development of downtown Wilmington and is, therefore, strongly opposed by this Board of Directors." Generously, the Board concluded by offering to help Cleancoal find "a more suitable terminal site."

Meanwhile, we were trying a new tack. Our "anti" group, called the Wilmington Improvement Committee, was gathering signatures on a petition that urged the City Council to acquire the proposed coal pile site for a convention center. (That would actually happen—but not for a couple more decades.)

All this time, I was spending countless hours trying to educate myself so we could intelligently answer the coal company's hired experts. I found an article in a technical journal called *Pollution Engineering* that detailed the environmental problems coal piles posed. The author explained how rainfall leaches toxic chemicals, including sulfuric acid, out of coal, creating "significantly polluted runoff," which must be captured and treated. "In other words," the article declared, "the existence of a coal pile means there is either a water pollution problem or a water treatment problem."

The author touched on "fugitive dust" moved by the wind, on noise from machinery, on serious fire hazards including spontaneous combustion, and on esthetics. "Coal piles are generally big, ugly, and dirty," the article concluded.

In September, a three-part *Morning Star* series gave Wilmington's newspaper readers a good sense of what to expect. These stories explained just how the east coast's biggest coal-export terminals operated, and how they affected the surrounding communities. Those were the enormous CSX operation at Newport News and the similar Norfolk & Western Railroad's terminal at Norfolk. One major difference was that the Virginia facilities, while much bigger than what Cleancoal planned for Wilmington, were also isolated within large port-authority tracts, so their impact on immediate neighbors was sharply reduced. Even so, one environmental activist who lived a mile from the Norfolk coal terminal said wind-blown coal dust was a problem even that far away.

The first story described what happened whenever a coal hopper was dumped at the Newport News terminal: "Black palls of dust obscured the entire outline of the tall dumper structure." It noted that transferring coal from railroad to ship "leaves a fine black layer on everything nearby: Buildings, cars and people."

Notably, neither of the huge Virginia operations included a coal "pile." As the story pointed out, "Neither railroad stores coal anywhere but in waiting hopper cars in sprawling classification yards, rather than large storage piles on the ground."

The series noted that some people appreciated the jobs and tax revenue the terminal provided, but that many other neighbors regretted the noise, the contamination, and the endless stream of coal trains.

The second story cited serious environmental problems that waiting coal ships had caused: "Oil spills, sewage leaks and blatant garbage dumping." The third piece in the series said officials in Virginia's port cities were most concerned about the impact of coal trains.

Pro and Con Opinions and a Likely Done Deal

All the evidence, both technical and common-sense, was clear: This project had no business being anywhere near downtown Wilmington. But even so, we couldn't find a way to stop it. Nor, it seemed, could the city government.

The City Council had at least been listening to our complaints. Just a day before my pitch to the DARE board, the Council had asked for a report on the coal pile's pros and cons.

City Manager Robert Cobb delivered that report two weeks later. He stated the city's obvious regulatory problem. The CSX site was zoned "M-1," which meant "light manufacturing." Under the city's zoning ordinance, Cobb wrote, "the proposed facility is a permitted use." That meant, he advised the Council, that it had few options. The city could do nothing, and we would get a coal pile downtown. Or it could try to impose a "moratorium" on building permits for coal-export facilities, which might stall the project until the land could be rezoned or, possibly, state or federal regulatory issues might stop the project.

But because the city "lacks express statutory authority" to impose building moratoriums, regardless of their purpose, Cobb warned that this tactic might get the city sued. Not only that, he said, but rezoning the site or amending the list of permitted uses in the zoning ordinance's "light manufacturing" classification could also lead to lawsuits. There was legal precedent: Property owners elsewhere had successfully argued that imposing new restrictions on how their land could be used amounted to the government "taking" their property without compensation.

Part of the city manager's report, echoing that *Pollution Engineering* article, offered predictions about what we could expect from an active coal terminal. The coal pile would be served by 300 trains a year, averaging almost six a week, each of them consisting of about 100 loaded hopper cars. "Total unit train length is in excess of one mile," Cobb noted. The Cleancoal proposal called for these trains to be broken up in CSX's Hilton Yards, just inside the city limits, and the coal shuttled downtown "in ten car 'cuts' between the coal facility and the staging area at Hilton Yards." (The track that would have served the site, by the way, ran through what is now the Pier 33 Apartments, the city's new Riverfront Park and Live Oak Pavilion, and the Sawmill Point Apartments.)

Concerning another potential impact, Cobb threw up his hands and admitted, "little information is available" on the actual noise levels from the coal-handling equipment proposed for the site. So despite documenting some of the potential problems, the city manager didn't exactly offer a ringing endorsement for trying to stop the project.

Just a week after Cobb delivered his report to the City Council, Cleancoal did more high-pressure lobbying of its own. The company sponsored a breakfast forum that was attended by some 400 business and community leaders. Many of them failed to recognize just what was at stake. Others saw benefits, at least to themselves, if the coal pile materialized.

The "pro" camp formed what they called "Citizens for Progress" to argue their case. Its leader was John T. "Tommy" Hale, who worked as a locomotive engineer for CSX. Besides the obvious fact that his employer owned the site, he foresaw immediate benefits for the railroad, predicting that it would have to create several hundred new jobs to serve the coal terminal. In November 1981, the *Morning Star* ran a feature about the controversy under the "Pro-Con" heading. On the "pro" side, Hale said, "This industry would be of great benefit to the local economy." He added, "It's hard for me to understand why people would want to keep out industry that would generate jobs." He also contended the coal pile would be all but invisible from downtown—at least as downtown was developed at the time—and so nothing to worry about.

In the same story, former County Commissioner Ellen Williams, who served on the county's Port, Waterway and Beach Commission, argued that the coal project would be good for the area's economy. She complained about what we had asked the City Council to do: "You have been asked to tell a private industry it cannot use its own property to make the most profit it can. That would hurt free enterprise."

On the City Council itself, the coal-pile boosters included William Schwartz and, after the 1981 election, E.A. Bordeaux. I was disappointed that Mayor Ben Halterman, who had played such a vital role in revitalizing downtown, said, "I happen to favor the river for the use of shipping, which includes coal." Like him, the newly elected Councilman Bordeaux would insist that the most appropriate place for a coal terminal was the downtown waterfront.

Then there was the business community.

Estell Lee, a leading member of the Chamber of Commerce, was president of Almont Shipping, which owned much of the land north of the coal pile site. No doubt she saw potential benefits for her company if CSX's adjacent industrial site could command a good price. She fought hard on Cleancoal's behalf, including directly lobbying the DARE Board of Directors. (It's ironic that the address of the Chamber's present-day headquarters, literally right next door to where the coal pile would have loomed, is 1 Estell Lee Place.)

It was after seeing what an influential figure like Lee could do that I concluded it was necessary to bring in some heavy guns of our own. That's why I got my father involved. As a former state representative, he was well suited to be the public face for the "anti" campaign. While I was executive director of the Wilmington Improvement Committee, the pressure group we formed, he was its president.

Of course, that also meant that he would be subject to lobbying from the "pro" faction. One prominent individual, one of my father's business partners, dismissed our worries that the coal pile would preclude any commercial or residential development on downtown's north end. That didn't matter, this gentleman told my father—because only Black people lived on Wilmington's north side.

Thankfully, some businesses took a longer view. One of DARE's biggest supporters in its early years was Rick Reeder, general manager of the Hilton hotel. That important establishment was barely 1,000 feet away from the site Cleancoal wanted to use. Just hours after Cleancoal's big breakfast meeting, Reeder wrote to his parent company, "The Hilton must discourage the use of this coal pile as it is incompatible with the downtown as a tourist and convention destination." Explaining the political and legal context, he added, "It appears to date the only way we can stop this development is to challenge the zoning statutes and block the City Council from issuing a building permit."

To be sure his corporate superiors understood how it affected their business, he said ". . . a four-story coal transfer pile with hundreds of railroad cars moving back and forth less than a quarter of a mile from the hotel on a twenty-four-hour, seven-day-a-week schedule is certainly not contributing to the Hilton clientele's quiet environment." He closed with this deft touch: Mentioning that CSX Railroad, which was planning to sell the site to Cleancoal, happened to own the swanky Greenbrier Hotel in White Sulfur Springs, W.Va., Reeder concluded, "I'll bet they wouldn't endorse a coal pile being built next to The Greenbrier."

Meanwhile, we (meaning DARE, my father, and a growing coalition of allies) were trying any tactics that showed any promise. Wearing my DARE hat, I tried to persuade the Army Corps of Engineers, which controlled permits for dredging and such, and the N.C. Division of Archives & History to put obstacles in Cleancoal's way. They couldn't (or a least didn't) help. In those days, it was said, the regulatory agencies in Gov. Jim Hunt's administration were routinely ready to "grease the skids" in favor of virtually any major industrial development.

I was able to enlist several strong voices to the cause. Groups that went on record against the coal pile included Residents of Old Wilmington, the Historic Wilmington Foundation, the environmentalists of Coastal Carolina Crossroads, and the Downtown Wilmington Association, the merchants' group. But even with this swelling chorus of anti-coal-pile voices behind us, our opposition wasn't getting any traction.

Finding a Loophole and Jumping through it

Public perception was important, of course. But what could we, or the public at large, do to actually stop the coal pile? The old ACL site's "light manufacturing" zoning was misleading. Yes, the M-1 zone wouldn't have permitted a blast furnace or an oil refinery. But the way the city zoning ordinance was worded, as Bob Cobb informed the City Council, it did permit a coal transfer facility. Allowed it "by right." That meant Cleancoal didn't even have to ask for the City Council's permission. No Planning Commission hearings; no rezonings or special-use permits; no public input of any kind.

Not that the Council would have stopped the coal pile even if it had the power. The city manager's pessimistic report about our prospects was typical; we got little encouragement from City Hall. Eager for economic development of any kind, regardless of its negative impacts on the community, a majority of the City Council was happy to welcome Cleancoal.

So despite plenty of vocal opposition, the coal pile was starting to look inevitable. Time was running out, and I was running out of ideas. I knew I had to do something; I didn't know what. Researching the city zoning ordinance was a bust; it offered no solutions. Next, I delved into Wilmington's City Charter and the relevant provisions of North Carolina law. I was looking for a loophole—and, unbelievably, I found it!

It was well after midnight one morning. As I remember, I was sipping on some Jack Daniel's. (It was that same elixir that Rick Willetts had poured out of a brown paper bag for me three years earlier, on that evening when he persuaded me to take the DARE job.)

In any case, the whiskey might have helped counteract the weariness I was feeling from reading through those tedious pages of legal procedure. And suddenly, in the middle of that dark night, I discovered something shocking. An obscure provision of the City Charter gave us a way to work around the City Council and the zoning ordinance. It turned out that Wilmington was one of a handful of North Carolina cities that allowed voters to initiate legislation through petition. And according to opinions from the N.C. Institute of Government, none of the cities with such charter provisions had ever made use of them. We would be the first.

This is how it would work: If we could get enough signatures on a petition, we could force the City Council to make a choice. It could directly change the City Code, specifically the part of the zoning ordinance that listed "permitted uses" in the M-1 light-industrial district. If the City Council didn't do that itself, it would have no choice but to call a public vote. Our first hurdle, then, was to draft a petition and get signatures. How many? The governing state law was clear: We needed twenty-five percent of the number of votes cast in the last "regular" city election. In those days, Wilmington held its election for mayor and council members in October. In 1981, only 5,164 people voted in that election. But because nobody won a majority for one of the Council seats, a November runoff was needed. Turnout for that would be even less, a mere 3,060. Was the runoff a "regular" election? Fortunately, we didn't have to decide that, since we were getting far more signatures than we needed. We used the larger turnout of the two 1981 Council elections. That meant we needed only 1,291 signatures.

Relying on that provision, we circulated our petition. It called for the Council to redefine the M-1 zone, which included the old railroad site, so coal terminals were no longer allowed there. The Council could either directly amend the zoning ordinance or call a special election and let Wilmington's voters decide.

It's worth pointing out that in listing the reasons a coal pile would "irreparably harm our city," our petition's final point was that by "removing a potentially ideal location for a Civic-Convention Center," it would interfere with job creation, tourist income, and tax revenue.

Beyond all the news coverage, we also benefitted from the *Morning Star*'s editorial support. An Oct. 30 editorial said, "It is, after all, the future of downtown Wilmington that is at stake. Will it be able to evolve into a tourism, convention, shopping and office center, or will a huge coal pile and shuttling coal trains, with their possible dust and noise, show or halt that progress? If our leaders won't lead, the people of Wilmington can. The future of downtown now appears to be up to them."

By signing this petition, Wilmington voters forced a referendum that decisively banned coal-shipping terminals from downtown.

Thanks in part to the sustained media attention to the "coal pile" issue, by the end of 1981 we had actually gotten over 1,800 signatures, far more than we needed. In January 1982, instead of immediately redefining the coal-pile site's zoning, the Council tossed the hot potato into voters' laps, calling for a referendum on the matter.

Finally, on June 29, 1982, voters got their say. By a nearly two-to-one ratio, 3,304 to 1,876, they said "No" to coal piles in the city's light industrial zones. That left the City Council with no choice. They had to do as the voters had ordered: Amend the M-1 zoning definition to ban "coal transfer faculties." The newspaper report from election night noted, "Councilman E.A. Bordeaux, who fought the zoning change, said he will abide by the will of the people and go along with the amendment." Even so, he said voters were confused by the ballot language, and doubled down on his belief that downtown was the best place for a coal pile.

Even after the people had spoken, we still worried that CSX, the railroad company that owned the site, would fight back. It might have argued that a forced "down zoning" infringed on its property rights. But CSX quickly announced that it wouldn't sue the city. And neither did Wilmington Coal Transfer, Inc., Cleancoal's North Carolina entity. By the following year, most of the other coal-export proposals had also quietly faded away. Demand for coal, which had spiked because of the cost of competing petroleum fuels, slacked off as international oil prices fell again.

We won the election, but more important—and time has proved this to be true—we saved downtown Wilmington. What would have been a coal yard is now a convention center and hotel. And along the rest of the northern riverfront, where those bulk-cargo warehouses once stood, locals and visitors alike now enjoy the Riverwalk, a public marina, upscale condos, restaurants, two concert venues, a city park, and a major office building. That former corporate headquarters is now home to Wilmington's city government—the same government that had to be forced to stop a major polluter from blighting our waterfront.

These developments' contributions to Wilmington and New Hanover County have included dramatically increased tourism, jobs, and tax revenue.

This movement could not have succeeded without the enthusiastic support of the city's good people, and I am proud to have been able to lead it. For a good while, of course, we didn't see any way to stop the coal pile. I credit "creativity" as our savior; I'm grateful to have found a creative solution to this serious problem. Before our petition drive and referendum, nobody else had ever taken advantage of that tactic, as state law and city charter allowed. We were the first!

Besides creativity, of course, it was dedication, persistence, and hard work that saved the day.

Long after we had won that battle, the *Morning Star* editorial page offered us a high compliment. Beginning with some comments about I-40, that November, 1984 opinion piece went on to say that my father and I "can take major credit for stopping a coal-loading terminal from being built on the downtown Wilmington waterfront."

It noted, accurately, that "The city staff and the City Council were perfectly happy to let that carbonaceous abomination be visited on a reviving downtown." And that we weren't. And that the city's voters had agreed with us, "overwhelmingly."

Gratifying as that praise from the editorial was, it was our fellow Wilmingtonians' votes to keep our waterfront unspoiled that really counted.

When it came to lobbying for highway construction, the author's father, Eugene Merritt, Sr., had excellent connections. Here he is, at right, during his 1979-81 term as a state representative, with Tom Bradshaw, Gov. Jim Hunt's secretary of transportation.

4. Interstate 40 to Wilmington

North Carolina had been a reluctant participant in the new Interstate Highway System. When President Dwight Eisenhower and Congress began that national highway network in 1956, many states hurried to join. North Carolina did not. Our state's leaders, suspicious of federal involvement in our affairs and fearful that costs would spiral out of control, lagged well behind their counterparts in adjacent Virginia, South Carolina, and Tennessee, all of which had eagerly taken advantage of the new federal Interstate dollars.

The only Interstates that North Carolina embraced in the program's first decades were those needed to link highways in those neighboring states: Interstates 95, 85, and 77 between Virginia and South Carolina, and the transcontinental Interstate 40. Tennessee was building its portion of that east-west route up to the state line in the Great Smoky Mountains. The North Carolina extension of I-40 was planned to link Tennessee with Asheville, Winston-Salem and Greensboro, where it would end at its junction with I-85. It would later be extended to Durham and, much later, to Raleigh. But for years the state's plans showed I-40 stopping there, at the capital city. Far from extending the rest of the way to the Atlantic Ocean, North Carolina's I-40 originally wasn't even meant to link with the East Coast's major north-south artery, Interstate 95.

And so matters remained by the mid-1970s. North Carolina's highway planners, firmly under the governor's control, had eventually accepted the need to at least connect the capital with I-95. Maps of that era showed double dashed lines extending east from Raleigh, in the general direction of Smithfield, representing the future completion of I-40. But nowhere in the state's seven-year Transportation Improvement Plan was there any high-speed highway to Wilmington and the southeastern coast.

Although it had been the state's biggest city until 1910, by 1975 Wilmington was isolated and hard to reach. Passenger rail service had petered out in 1968. Our air service consisted mostly of Piedmont Airlines' two-engine prop-driven planes, which typically flew short hops to other cities in the region. Vacationers from as nearby as Raleigh preferred to take their beach holidays on the Bogue Banks near Morehead City. The highways in that direction were better, including several long four-lane stretches. Wilmington's State Port was struggling to compete with its rivals in Norfolk, Va. and Charleston, S.C., both of which had Interstate Highway links. In fact, North Carolina was the only state whose deep-water port wasn't linked to the Interstate system. In an industry where time is money, shippers were reluctant to commit to using a port that was costly, slow, and inefficient for trucks to access.

* * *

I knew that all too well. In the mid-1970s, after I'd started my public relations firm, I decided I needed better exposure and a guaranteed paycheck. So I took the position of director of advertising and public relations for the N.C. State Ports Authority, which runs both the Wilmington and Morehead City ports. By getting to know its management staff, I learned a lot about the SPA's operational needs. In those years, the biggest trend in shipping was containerization. Instead of hoisting cargo piecemeal in nets, requiring lots of handling by human stevedores, shippers were increasingly packing their wares in standardized containers that were easily transferred from trucks and trains to ships, and vice versa. But the "easily" part had a catch: Moving those big forty-foot containers between ship and shore required specialized cranes. And North Carolina's ports didn't have any.

Also growing more and more important was finding efficient land routes for moving these containers. The rail option had much less potential than trucking, I learned. My managers told me that an Interstate Highway from Wilmington to Raleigh would be a major game-changer, not just for our port, but for the whole state. This mindset stayed with me even after I left the SPA; it guided my drive to get I-40 completed to Wilmington. And, in retrospect, I can say the freeway was, indeed, the game changer my Port Authority managers had predicted.

The politics of the ports, however, were an education themselves, and gave me a taste of what we would contend with in getting the Interstate Highway built.

In the 1970s, a powerful legislator, State Senator Livingstone Stallings from New Bern, represented Morehead City. While his support for the port in his district was only natural, it came with harsh opposition to anything that might benefit Wilmington. He frankly resented the idea of doing anything to expand the port here. Stallings had continuously made very personal and negative comments about the management and operations of the Port of Wilmington.

After the SPA Board decided to invest in the future and buy two specialized container cranes, Stallings used his influence to overrule the SPA's experts and ensure that only one of them would come to Wilmington. The second crane was earmarked for Morehead City, even though that port—then as now—handled almost exclusively bulk cargoes, and no container traffic. After its delivery at the end of 1976, that politically positioned crane sat idle on the Morehead City waterfront for several years, a testament to the perils of political meddling. Finally, the political climate improved and it was moved to Wilmington, where it should have been in the first place.

State Senator Livingstone Stallings of New Bern

Reacting to all this, I may have overstepped my role as a state agency's PR man. But after seeing Stallings' attacks on the Wilmington port in the local newspapers, I personally chastised him. I was quoted as calling him a "traitor" to the state of North Carolina.

Stallings used his power in Raleigh to get me fired in September 1977.

For me, that was just as well. The same day I was fired in Wilmington, I accepted the job of special assistant to state Secretary of Cultural Resources Sara Hodgkins. That helped me decide what my working future would look like. During my tenure with Cultural Resources, I was able to complete some quality work and put some new ideas into play.

And then came my four-plus years with DARE and downtown Wilmington, which I've already described.

* * *

All this time, however, I'd been involved in Democratic Party politics. It wasn't just me; it was also my father and my brother John. We had helped Charlie Rose get elected to Congress for the first time, in 1972. Recognizing that, Rose had hired John, first to run his Wilmington office, but eventually as his chief of staff. John would serve in that role until 1982, amassing significant contacts on the local, state, and federal levels.

Meanwhile, my other brother, Steve, was working in Raleigh for Secretary of Transportation Tom Bradshaw, in the state's aviation division.

And in 1978, my father was elected to represent New Hanover County in the state House of Representatives.

* * *

So in our family alone, we had established a valuable network of political contacts who could assist with our desire to get I-40 finished, linking Wilmington to Raleigh and the rest of the nation. Without those contacts, we could not have succeeded in gaining the funds and approvals needed to build the road.

Several of those contacts—allies, even—deserve special mention.

Billy Rose (no relation to Charlie) was the state DOT's liaison with the federal government. He played an important role in the process and was very helpful in our cause.

Jim Hunt, who became governor in 1977, was also very helpful to us in getting the freeway started. Later, unfortunately, he tried to play politics with funds that should have finished I-40's construction. He decided that spreading those dollars around the state, to help his prospects in the 1984 U.S. Senate election, was more important than getting our freeway finished. By 1984, Hunt's highway funding plans would have put off I-40's completion by a full ten years.

Earlier, such allies as Billy Rose and Jim Hunt had helped us get the project under way. But by the mid-'80s, the most important matter was finding the money to complete the last ninety miles to Wilmington.

For that, we found saviors in Congress. In the final analysis, it was our own Charlie Rose, along with U.S. Rep. Bill Hefner—who represented a southern Piedmont district—who got us the money and made it all possible.

But before I get back to the political maneuverings in Raleigh and Washington—and here in Wilmington—it's important to explain just how important it was to get that road built.

You Can't Get There from Here

Anyone who first came to Wilmington after 1990 may have trouble understanding what it was once like traveling to or from here. Today, to get to Raleigh, a Wilmington resident need only merge onto I-40 from northbound College Road, and in less than two hours will arrive in the capital. Traveling northbound on I-95, toward Richmond, or Washington, or anyplace in the Northeast? At seventy miles an hour, it's just an hour and a half on I-40 to its interchange with I-95.

Now imagine what it was like before our freeway was built.

Some motorists chose to go north on Castle Hayne Road (then U.S. 117), or on North College Road, N.C. 132, until those two-lane roads merged just inside the county line. Then, for the next fifty-five miles, they would stay on two-lane Route 117—frequented by school buses, tractors and other slow-moving farm machines—through a long string of small towns. Each of those slowed down through travelers with thirty-five-m.p.h. speed limits, local traffic, and stoplights. Then, after passing the last of those bottlenecks at Faison, still only halfway to Raleigh, those travelers would turn onto N.C. 50, which meanders through the tobacco and cucumber fields of Duplin and Sampson Counties. Somewhere past the crossroads called Suttontown, the route changed to N.C. 55, which took motorists to the roundabout in tiny Newton Grove. There, they picked up U.S. 701. That two-lane route extended as far as I-95 near Smithfield, from which point U.S. 301 and U.S. 70 eventually took those weary travelers into Raleigh.

Others in Wilmington favored one or more 421 options. Those involved crossing the Northeast Cape Fear River on a rickety two-lane drawbridge dating from 1929, then following U.S. 421 north, past where its short four-lane section reverted to two lanes, and on through sparsely populated rural territory to the town of Clinton. There, miraculously, 421 became a four-lane freeway for a few miles. That break from two-lane roads was evidence of how powerful legislators, such as Clinton's own D.M. "Lauch" Faircloth (later a U.S. senator), had always managed to steer highway money toward their home towns, regardless of need. It was no coincidence that prominent signs reminded drivers they were on the "Faircloth Freeway."

Those few miles of freeway ran out soon enough, though, leaving travelers a choice. They could branch off up U.S. 701, the Smithfield route to I-95 and Raleigh, or stay on 421 for a few more two-lane miles. Just past Spivey's Corner, savvy travelers would veer off on N.C. 242, then switch to

N.C. 50 near Benson, and follow that two-lane until hitting U.S. 70 in the suburbs of Raleigh, which would take them the rest of the way into the big city.

First elected to Congress in 1972, Charlie Rose represented Southeastern North Carolina until 1993.

It was that simple!

No wonder tourists had to be seriously motivated even to attempt a vacation in Wilmington or at any of our nearby beach communities. No wonder truckers hated having to haul cargoes to or from our handful of industrial plants, or to the State Port. No wonder would-be industrial developers looked askance at a place where their supply chains would inevitably get bogged down on the inadequate highway connections.

In simple terms, this intolerable situation existed because of political mathematics. Wilmington and nearby communities didn't have anywhere near the numbers of voters as the state's bigger urban centers. And having fairly competitive politics, we never managed to elect anybody quite like those long-serving legislators who amassed serious power in the General Assembly. That power allowed those lawmakers—like Lauch Faircloth—to reliably steer road dollars to their own districts. Besides the finite state transportation budget, funded from fuel taxes, available federal money was caught in a Catch-22. Potential federal matching money for Interstate Highway construction depended on the state designating a project as an Interstate. Yet the state showed little or no interest in doing so, except in the voter-rich communities already served by Interstates, or those like Raleigh for which the I-40 link to points west was still pending in the '70s.

Governor Jim Hunt first put the I-40 extension in the state's seven-year Transportation Improvement Plan.

Wilmington had been through something similar in the decades before.

Frustrated that our only bridges across the Cape Fear River's two branches were outdated and overloaded, the community had been agitating for a new bridge for years. Finally, in 1963, a bus caravan of our region's business and government leaders descended on Raleigh to personally lobby legislators. That pressure campaign ultimately paid off when the four-lane Cape Fear Memorial Bridge opened in 1969.

But ten years later, virtually no new major highway projects had come to this corner of the state. The chief exception was U.S. 74-76, which leads westward from the Cape Fear Memorial Bridge. Scattered portions were widened to four lanes in the '70s, but for many years to come, most of that road remained two lanes.

In those years, too, the industries that had begun to transform Wilmington's economy, the likes of DuPont, General Electric, and Corning, were feeling the need for better transportation connections.

Charlie Rose was a natural ally. When he first ran unsuccessfully for Congress in 1970, the real contest came in the Democratic primary against the incumbent, U.S. Rep. Alton Lennon. On his boss's behalf, my brother John reminded *Morning Star* readers in December 1983, "Rose made an issue when he ran against Alton that the area was not served by an interstate." He also asserted that in the 1972 election, which put Rose in Congress, "That was the litmus test: Were you for the highway?" In retrospect, John admitted, that assertion was largely after-the-fact "spin"—really, the highway had been a minor issue in Rose's 1972 campaign.

But that year's election had also given us a new governor, the first to get serious about building a four-lane highway to Wilmington. Jim Holshouser, North Carolina's first Republican governor since 1901, established the first statewide Transportation Improvement Plan, which included widening part of U.S. 421. That's how that highway's first, and only, few dozen four-lane miles got built from Wilmington up into Pender County. But when Jim Hunt replaced Holshouser in the Governor's Mansion in 1977, the money allocated for U.S. 421 was diverted to U.S. 264, which just happens to connect Raleigh with Hunt's home town, Wilson. Also that year, despite a state attempt to get an official Interstate designation for a freeway to Wilmington, the federal DOT said "No." That meant we couldn't get the favorable 90/10 federal/state funding ratio for Interstates. Instead, any such project would fall under the 75/25 ratio that applies to virtually all other federal-aid highway work.

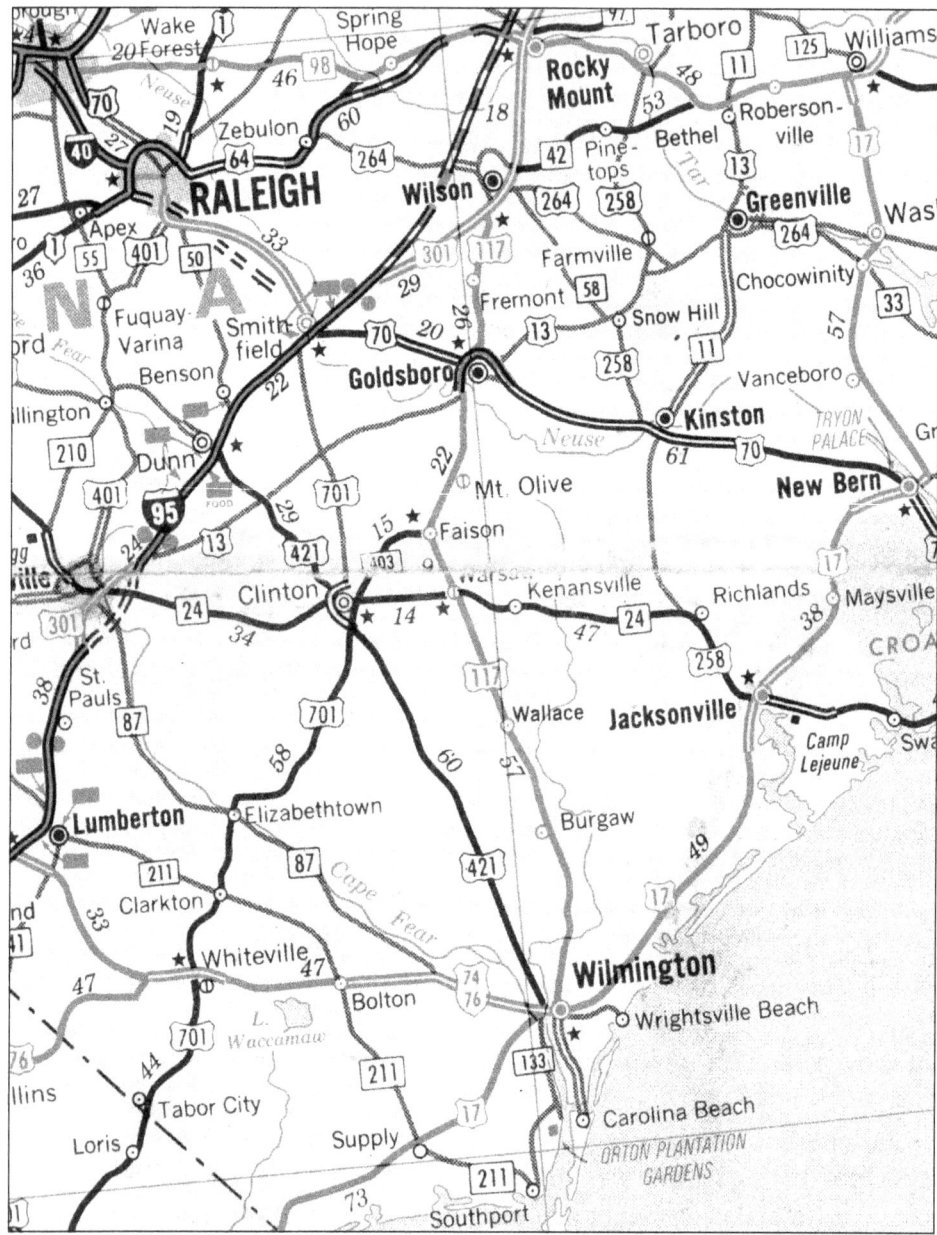

Double dashed lines on this 1977 Exxon road map show how I-40's proposed extension from Raleigh was planned to meet I-95 near Smithfield. Had it been built that way, any future interstate highway to the Atlantic coast would almost certainly have followed U.S. 70 toward New Bern and Morehead City. Bending the Raleigh-to-I-95 route southward, to the vicinity of Benson, was a prerequisite to ultimately getting the freeway built to Wilmington.

* * *

A critical early fight concerned the extension of I-40 from Raleigh to I-95, which had been approved in 1969 but was still unbuilt. As originally proposed, it would have connected to I-95 near Smithfield or Selma, more or less easterly from the capital. Any further extension from that point to the coast would most logically have gone on east toward New Bern and Morehead City. Not southerly; not to Wilmington. For a time, state DOT officials were considering upgrading the already mostly four-lane U.S. 70 and designating it as I-40. Had that happened, it would have been fatal to our region's hopes.

That's where we did get an essential boost from Jim Hunt and his allies. Even before the first dollar had been allocated for a freeway to the coast, the state had to decide where to terminate I-40's already approved extension to I-95.

This led to a major battle to reroute the proposed Raleigh-to-I-95 link so it ended near the small Johnston County town of Benson. From that point, a southerly extension to Wilmington would be feasible. We lobbied to get that route altered to make Benson the terminus. From there, a freeway extension would be essentially a straight shot to Wilmington.

In 1977, the Wilmington City Council, Carolina Beach Town Council, and the New Hanover County Commissioners all passed resolutions in favor of the Benson route.

Also that year, a consultant was preparing a report for the state that outlined the pros and cons of several potential freeway routes. It included five different tracks for the Raleigh-to-I-95 stretch, and half a dozen alternatives for a possible extension to Wilmington. In November, a busload of people from the Wilmington area packed a Raleigh meeting of the Board of Transportation, though they didn't get an opportunity to speak. A news story about this quoted William G. Broadfoot Jr., speaking for our Chamber of Commerce. He put the issue bluntly. "If it goes to Smithfield, they're not going to turn it and bring it into Wilmington."

We got the chance to speak in February 1978, when the state DOT held a pair of hearings about where the Raleigh-to-I-95 link should go. A session in Benson drew a standing-room-only crowd of about 600, twice as many as attended the parallel hearing in Smithfield. Somewhere around a hundred Wilmington-area residents attended the Benson hearing. Folks from here didn't neglect the Smithfield hearing, either. Those who spoke argued that routing I-40 to Smithfield would cost truckers extra mileage and congestion, and a significant loss of travel time. One of the speakers was New Hanover County Commissioner Ellen Williams. She said, "We feel the more southern the route, the more beneficial to the Wilmington area," and the more likely that a future I-40 extension would come in our direction.

A month later, when the Board of Transportation met in Wilmington, it was already leaning toward the Benson routing. The *Morning Star*'s report again summarized the issue: "An I-40 link at Benson would mean future extension of I-40 would be more likely to come directly toward Wilmington."

But there was no obvious source of federal funding for the next ninety miles to Wilmington. State DOT officials seemed resigned to a long wait before our freeway could get built. The same story touched on that: "They are counting heavily on U.S. Rep. Charles Rose . . . to find those Interstate funds in Washington, D.C." But the immediate need, as the story concluded, was "to win the battle over the I-40 route, since it is the first step."

It was April 21, 1978 when the Board of Transportation voted unanimously to make Benson the junction point for I-40 and I-95. The board also agreed that any future extension of I-40 would run roughly parallel to U.S. 117, instead of being an upgrade to the U.S. 421 corridor.

That decision followed recommendations from the state's consulting engineers. Their reasoning included the better federal-state funding ratio available for an Interstate Highway compared to improving an existing road. Instead of shouldering twenty-five percent of the cost of widening 421, the state would pay only ten percent of the all-new Interstate route's cost. Still to be determined, though, was where to find that other ninety percent.

During this time, Charlie Rose was, indeed, stepping up to secure the needed federal funding. In May 1978, he promised a Chamber of Commerce delegation in Washington that he would call in all the favors his congressional colleagues owed him.

So by the end of 1978, the vital first battle had been won. I-40 would go to Benson, and the stretch between there and Raleigh had been allocated $87 million for design and construction. Most important, the state Board of Transportation finally put the proposed coastal extension, from Benson to Wilmington, in the seven-year TIP. It would be built to Interstate Highway standards, the plan said. When finished, it would be designated Interstate 40, the plan promised. And its route paralleling U.S. 117 put the freeway close to a string of small towns. That was in line with Gov. Hunt's "Balanced Growth" policies, which aimed to stimulate growth in those nearby communities. Those included Burgaw and Wallace, Warsaw and Kenansville, Rose Hill and Magnolia—my father's home town.

There was just that one little problem: The money. That's why our freeway was listed in the very back pages of the thick TIP book, and designated by the strange abbreviation "X-3." As in algebra, that "X" represented an unknown quantity. Unknown in this case: How are we going to pay for this?

But after putting X-3 in the TIP, Jim Hunt's Board of Transportation wasn't likely to be much help in finding the money. Nor were his allies in the General Assembly. Why? Partly, I believe, because in those days Wilmington and New Hanover County were out of step with the state government. And unlike such places as Clinton, where long-serving legislators had amassed clout over decades, our General Assembly delegation seemed to change with nearly every election.

When 1979 began, my father had just begun his term as a state representative. As with most freshman legislators, he had limited influence in the House. He and our region's other legislators would do what they could in Raleigh, but it was clear that we also needed allies in Washington.

Finding the Federal Funding

In February 1979, the *Sunday Star-News* published its annual "Progress" economic-review supplement. One major story projected that I-40 would be finished from Wilmington to Raleigh by 1986. That optimistic schedule was based in part on the U.S. Department of Transportation's recent approval of $20 million to be used to start buying right of way, and a February 1979 state agreement to add another $3 million to that. At the time, state DOT officials were projecting a total cost of $180 million.

That piece quoted an NCDOT report from the previous year. It stated that a lack of four-lane highways "has been a sore point with the people of eastern North Carolina for years." Without a good connection to Wilmington's port, the DOT said, truckers and shippers were reluctant to provide service here. Most of North Carolina's exports went out through Norfolk, Va., or Charleston, S.C. Both industrial recruiting and tourism were directly harmed, the DOT report added.

That same article quoted me as saying, "Wilmington has always seemed to have an antagonistic attitude toward Raleigh. That has been to our detriment."

And that's why, with only faint support from the state, we'd had to look to the federal government. This is how that played out.

It was late 1978 when Charlie Rose got to work. He and his fellow North Carolina congressman, Rep. W.G. "Bill" Hefner, took note of an important fact about federal highway funding: Peculiarities in the federal formulas for returning fuel-tax dollars to the states had left North Carolina deeply in the hole. As Billy Rose, the state's administrator for federal highways never tired of arguing, we were getting back a smaller proportion of that money than almost any other state, only sixty-two cents for every federal tax dollar our motorists paid at the gas pump.

Congressman Bill Hefner was one of Charlie Rose's chief allies in his work to get federal funds for I-40.

John Merritt, the author's brother, was Congressman Rose's chief of staff during the I-40 funding fight.

"The key guy here was Billy Rose," was my brother John's assessment. Rose's case that North Carolina was a "donor state" and was "getting screwed" on the funding formulas had gotten some sympathy within the federal DOT. But attempts to adjust how gas tax money was distributed ran into a roadblock in Congress. In those days, the joint appropriations committee that governed such matters was dominated by long-serving congressmen from New Jersey, which was enjoying the opposite situation: Getting back more highway dollars than it contributed. Bill Hefner tried to make some headway there, with no success. "They kept beating Hefner like a rented mule," was how John described it, "and blocking us."

* * *

But in the course of meetings involving our friends in Congress and the state's lobbyists in Washington, Billy Rose had mentioned something important. As an end run around the normal highway funding system, some influential lawmakers had created a $120 million "discretionary fund," which had already committed money to two highway projects. Both of them were "to be named for powerful people," as John recalled it. As it turned out, those two projects hadn't used up all the money in that fund.

That would soon change, thanks in part to Billy Rose's carefully cultivated contacts in the federal DOT, and in part to Charlie Rose's alliance with then-House Speaker Tip O'Neill. Jimmy Carter's secretary of transportation, Brock Adams, designated our X-3 freeway, the I-40 extension, as that discretionary fund's third project.

Besides the value of the money, this had one other major benefit: Unlike most federal highway dollars, these couldn't be used for anything but the I-40 extension. In other words, Jim Hunt's Board of Transportation couldn't pull a budgetary switcheroo, like how it had once abandoned the U.S. 421 widening in favor of U.S. 264. The discretion lay with the U.S. secretary of transportation, not with the governor's people. From his vantage point in Charlie Rose's office, John explained it like this: "We provided dollars out of the sphere of political influence. They were directed to X-3 and that alone. They could not be subjected to the transportation board members, who are only interested in doing projects in their own areas."

Suddenly, with serious federal money at hand, North Carolina's highway officials got seriously busy. Already, as Jim Hunt later made a point of taking credit for, his administration had come up with that $3 million in matching state money, enough to hire engineers and start designing the freeway. That allowed construction to start promptly once federal funds actually started flowing.

And so, in early 1979, the money began to flow. John recalls going to Raleigh to see our brother Steve, whose office was just two doors down from Billy Rose's. During that visit, he encountered NCDOT head Tom Bradshaw, who gave John a bear hug and announced, "We got a check for $20 million this morning!"

After that tap opened, Carter's discretionary fund would ultimately provide $60 million. That, along with $40 million that the state would spend up to 1983, got all design work finished and all rights of way purchased. By then, construction had begun on thirty-five of the ninety miles between

Wilmington and Benson. Before we reached that milestone, however, we would have a lot of bumpy road to travel.

By 1980, the economy was in trouble. Inflation had been a problem for years. The Iran hostage crisis had triggered a new spike in oil prices. Motorists were driving fewer miles, buying less fuel, and contributing fewer tax dollars to the state's highway fund.

The elections that year drastically changed the political landscape, too. Ronald Reagan defeated Jimmy Carter. And soon, Reagan's allies in Congress, including our own Senator Jesse Helms, were threatening to abolish Carter's special highway fund.

That didn't sit well with people here in Wilmington, including a group generally sympathetic to Reagan's conservative, pro-business policies: The Chamber of Commerce. In April 1981, just three months into the Reagan administration, Federal Highway Administrator Ray Barnhart spoke to the Chamber, where he attempted to justify turning off the highway-money tap.

Barnhart contended that North Carolina could still finance the I-40 extension without the fund the administration and its Congressional allies were about to kill. The business leaders in the audience weren't buying it.

Robert Warwick, the commercial real-estate broker who was the Chamber's president that year, said he and other business people planned to do some in-person lobbying in Washington, urging our Congressional delegation to keep some form of I-40 funding in the federal budget. "It's going to take all the North Carolina delegation to keep this money in the system," Warwick said at the time. He clarified that he was mostly talking about Jesse Helms and our other Republican senator, John East. That required some wishful thinking. "Sen. Helms has not been critical of the highway," Warwick insisted. "He's been critical of the method of funding the highway."

Soon enough, Helms's own words would say otherwise. And a year later, Bob Warwick would join with us to form the NC I-40 group.

At that stage, Governor Hunt was struggling to cope with slumping gas tax revenues and threatened cuts in federal support. On March 2, he wrote me to say, "You know how strongly I support I-40 to Wilmington, and I will do everything I can to see that it is completed. I cannot, of course, predict what action the Reagan Administration might take that would affect this."

Meanwhile, we could still count on strong support from Charlie Rose. Month after month, as John recalled, the congressman's staff "had been beating the drum" about I-40 in his monthly newsletter. It was mailed to some 8,000 people in New Hanover County, including most of our movers and shakers. Between what my father and I were arguing locally, and what Rose kept reminding his constituents about, Wilmington's business community was primed to ask some tough questions.

This happened at that April Chamber of Commerce meeting with Reagan's highway chief. John attended on Charlie Rose's behalf. Afterward, he told the *Morning Star*, "That was a fairly hostile crowd." He elaborated, "Barnhart was trying to play with the group last night, trying to suggest to them that North Carolina was going to get the same amount of dollars that it was before. That's just not accurate." In fact, John said, the state's share of the federal Highway Trust Fund would drop from $199 million in 1981 to just $131 million the next year, under Reagan's first budget.

"When Rose can," John said about his boss, "he will work on it day or night. It just makes it easier when you've got somebody helping him." But from the Senate, he added, Charlie Rose hadn't gotten any help. Still, he hoped Helms and East wouldn't actively fight against funding the freeway. "If they're not going to help, we don't want them to obstruct, either."

At least one of our senators did, in fact, obstruct.

Helms would prove a particularly troublesome foe. He wasn't just objecting to details of funding, as Jim Hunt would later do, too. No, contrary to Bob Warwick's optimistic view, Helms was adamantly opposed to the idea of building I-40 *at all*. His stated objection was that it would take land away from farmers. He made that argument even though his preferred alternative, widening U.S. 421, would not only have taken farmland, but also condemned homes and businesses by the hundreds. Helms' real objection was that building the freeway would help Jim Hunt. "Even then," John would say in 1983, "Helms was setting himself up as the opposite to Hunt."

John still believes that. Helms' objective, he said recently, was to oppose "anything that would help Hunt." Decades earlier, of course, as an aggressive political

Senator Jesse Helms opposed the I-40 extension to Wilmington, favoring widening U.S. 421 instead.

operative, John routinely characterized Helms' position as flat-out opposition to our highway. He acknowledges today that "Senator 'No's" stance on I-40 was more partisan rhetoric than active interference.

Helms' protégé, Sen. John East, was a slightly different story. Sometimes called "Helms on Wheels" because he used a wheelchair, he largely echoed his senior colleague's positions. But on this issue, East broke with his mentor, giving at least some lip service to I-40.

U.S. Senator John East made some favorable statements about I-40.

Helms doubled down, at least rhetorically. After the New Hanover County Commissioners appealed to the senator to support federal funding for the freeway, Helms responded dismissively. In a Nov. 16, 1981 letter, the senator tried to have things both ways. On the one hand, he said the I-40 project cost too much, and called it "ill-advised" and "wasteful." On the other hand, he disavowed any responsibility for it, saying neither he nor any other federal official could get the highway built or block it. "The decisions on this project, and all other highway projects in North Carolina, are made in Raleigh, not Washington."

And so despite his support of Reagan's action to kill the Carter-administration discretionary fund, Helms said the state "will continue to receive federal highway money."

One rebuttal to that, of course, came from Charlie Rose. He noted, as John did after that Chamber meeting, that the almost $200 million in federal highway funds the state got in the last year Jimmy Carter was president would be cut by $70 million under Reagan's proposed budget for 1982. Furthermore, Rose argued, North Carolina's normal allocation represented a return of only sixty-two cents on every gas-tax dollar the state sent to Washington. The soon-to-be-abolished discretionary fund had helped reduce that imbalance.

Eventually, though, in December 1981, Congress reached a compromise between the Senate, which wanted to kill the discretionary fund immediately, and the House, which wanted to enlarge it. The compromise would keep the $125 million pot of money unchanged, for one final year.

Getting Our Slice from a Shrinking State Pie

With federal funds suddenly in jeopardy, the state's gasoline-tax revenues were falling short of what was needed just to finish highways already in the Transportation Improvement Plan. Hunt's DOT officials were asking the legislature for a five-cents-per-gallon tax increase. In February 1981, the Board of Transportation member from our corner of the state, Garland B. Garrett Jr., said, "It doesn't take a genius to say we're in critical shape from the standpoint of funding. If something isn't done about that, then there's no use of talking about the future."

That year, the state was planning to spend a bit less than $52 million toward I-40's total price tag, which by then had risen to $293 million. The General Assembly agreed to bump up the gasoline tax, but by only three cents instead of the five the state DOT wanted. That left highway projects squeezed all over the state.

Our local officials pleaded with the state to keep I-40 on schedule.

In early April 1981, around the time Ray Barnhart spoke to the Chamber, the Wilmington Area Transportation Advisory Committee voted to put I-40 at the top of the region's highway priority list.

A week later, the NCDOT held a hearing in Wilmington. The businessman Pete Fensel, who was chairman of the Wilmington Highway Priorities Task Force, told DOT officials that the freeway extension would be "economically helpful to the entire state." At the same meeting, we got support from our friends up the road. Wilbur Hussey, who was chairman of the Duplin County Industrial Board, called I-40 "vital to southeastern North Carolina and Duplin County." The chief reply from the DOT people at the hearing was to reiterate that the state's highway plan had run head-on into a financial crisis, aggravated by rising construction costs and falling gas-tax revenues.

No amount of public support for a future freeway could solve the state's fuel-tax problem. The transportation-funding pot was shrinking, and hard decisions had to be made.

In December 1981, Hunt's Board of Transportation slashed $1.2 billion from the seven-year TIP, eliminating a full third of the highway projects that had been planned for the rest of the decade. That pushed the completion date for I-40 back from 1986 to 1990. Virtually every other highway project in our region was canceled entirely. That's why, for example, it would take another two decades and more to get the present Martin Luther King Parkway and the I-140 Outer Loop Freeway built.

And immediately after that, to nobody's surprise, Congress abolished the Carter-era federal discretionary fund.

North Carolina wasn't the only state left in the lurch when that fund was killed. Congressmen from other "donor" states were raising Cain, too. By 1982, pressure on Congress from many directions had resulted in a new funding opportunity, directed toward the same projects the repealed fund had helped. This was the creation of a new category, "primary priority" highways, that could now qualify for an especially sweet ninety-five/five federal-to-state funding ratio.

The key point, of course, was that our Project X-3 had been defined as one of those "primary priority" routes. That was great news. But it would also open up one of the toughest fights of all, one that would require all our political and public-relations skills to win. By now, the chief issue was how Jim Hunt's administration was allocating its shrunken pot of transportation money. Getting the I-40 extension started, he apparently concluded, had solidified his support from our corner of the state. That meant he could turn his attention, and substantial highway spending, in other directions.

Amid all the uncertainties in both Washington and Raleigh, some of us in Wilmington concluded that we needed to work harder to keep the money coming, and to keep the pressure on our elected representatives. By 1982, that pressure did seem to be paying off.

State Senator J.A. 'Chip' Wright of New Hanover County

For example, during the 1980 election, Republican candidates for our area's legislative seats had criticized Democrats for concentrating too much on I-40. But over the next couple of years, they changed their tune. For example, State Sen. Julius A. "Chip" Wright, first elected in 1980, wrote a letter to the *Morning Star*'s editor the following April, urging "concerned citizens" to contact Helms, East, and Hunt. Calling I-40 "of immense importance" to the region, he said, "The fate of this highway is resting in the hands" of those officials. "It is incumbent upon the citizens of Southeastern North Carolina to bombard these gentlemen with letters in support of I-40." He called for "A deluge of letters coming from citizens, business, industry, concerned groups, etc.," to let the senators and the governor know how most voters feel about the highway. "We need to prove to Raleigh and Washington that we have twenty voters who want I-40 for every one who doesn't," Wright concluded.

When 1982 began, the rest of our Republican legislators were firmly in the pro-I-40 camp, too. And even Charlie Rose's Republican opponent for Congress that year, a protégé and ally of Jesse Helms, tried to pretend he was, too. He postured to the effect that, in some way he never specified, he could do better than Rose at getting the money needed to finish the freeway. He went so far as to call a "press conference" in the middle of the freeway's under-construction right of way, hoping to steal freeway supporters' votes away from his opponent. It didn't work. Rose was comfortably re-elected and continued to work on our behalf.

That summer, amid positive developments from Washington, and continued foot-dragging in Raleigh, we decided to incorporate our informal pressure group as "NC I-40, Inc." I was its president; Bob Warwick was vice president. Other incorporators were my father and a politically active Pender County physician, Dr. John Dees. We started with a proposed budget of $35,000, small even in those days for a lobbying group, though it did eventually rise to $86,500 before we were through. Our objective was to keep up unrelenting public pressure on all our legislators, both state and federal, as well as on Governor Hunt's administration.

NC I-40 worked to recruit support from all communities along the I-40 route. We met with the city councils and town boards; with boards of county commissioners; with chambers of commerce and economic development organizations. For their own good reasons, the business and political leaders of Pender, Duplin, Sampson, and Johnston Counties—the entire route between here and I-95—were just as eager as we were to get the freeway finished. We also directly lobbied state legislators, Board of Transportation members, and the congressmen whose districts included the highway's route.

Many of those meetings included significant public participation. To further rally public opinion, we dug into our pockets to print and distribute thousands of bumper stickers. In white type on a black background, they read: "I-40 Benson to Wilmington."

Bumper stickers were an important part of the NC I-40, Inc. campaign to raise public awareness and put pressure on state officials to get the freeway fully funded and construction finished without endless delays.

Playing Games in the Legislature

While our message started turning up on cars across the region, we also established a speaker's bureau to help spread our message. Other communication efforts included letters to the editors of newspapers along the route: Not just Wilmington's *Morning Star* but also weekly papers in places like Burgaw and Wallace and Clinton. We did radio and TV interviews. All that helped sway popular opinions, as did a steady stream of news coverage in the *Morning Star* and *Sunday Star-News*.

"Our main goal," the *Star-News* quoted me in its February 1983 "Progress" supplement, "is to make sure on a state level that this road remains the priority primary and that the state does indeed carry through with its commitment to finish this road." I was determined to remain a squeaky wheel, especially with the powers that be in Raleigh. "As things change, people change," I told the newspaper. "Things have a way of being forgotten sometimes and we're not going to let this situation be forgotten. We are going to keep reminding people of the commitment we have to build a road."

Within a year after the new federal "primary priority" funding became available, the freeway had gotten nearly $10 million from that pot of federal money, which required a match of just half a million state dollars. But even through construction was well under way, our governor decided it would be better for him (if not for the state, as he claimed) if he steered the state's matching money in different directions.

Here's how it played out in the spring of 1983. The new federal funding source had been enacted on the basis of partially leveling the nationwide playing field for highway building. The bill that provided this had aimed to ensure that states got back a fairer percentage of the gasoline taxes they sent to Washington, at eighty-five cents per dollar. That's how North Carolina got another special allocation, $24.9 million each of the next two years. But then came the tricky part: How to use state money to match those federal dollars.

The beauty of this legislation was that its generous ratio of just five state dollars for every ninety-five federal dollars applied only for so-called "primary priority" projects. And, as our allies in Washington had worked out, the I-40-to-Wilmington project was the only one in this state that qualified for that most-favorable funding formula.

If that federal money was used for any other highways, the state would have to come up with the normal twenty-five-percent match. In other words, if these dollars, almost twenty-five million of them a year, were used for anything but I-40, it would cost the state another $7 million a year, or $14 million altogether. And that's exactly what Gov. Jim Hunt wanted to do: Spend the new money on a range of projects across the state, despite the extra cost. Challenged in April 1983 about why that money shouldn't go toward I-40, he answered, "That would be fine if you believe it outweighs all the other projects in the state."

From Hunt's point of view, it made far better sense to spread that money around, despite the less-favorable matching formula, to places where it could earn him more votes.

Term limits meant Hunt couldn't run for governor again. But he was already planning to seek Jesse Helms' Senate seat in the 1984 election. For an ambitious politician like Hunt, every ribbon-cutting ceremony for a new road project represented another bloc of potential votes. So of course he wanted total freedom to allocate those highway funds as he saw fit.

But he wasn't the only politician with a say in this. The General Assembly could decide to steer those nearly 25 million federal dollars to the I-40 project and take advantage of the better matching ratio. Altogether, we were pushing to allocate a total of $53.4 million in federal funds for I-40 over the next two-year state budget cycle. That would have gotten us about a quarter of the way to completion; roughly $200 million was needed to build the rest of the ninety-mile freeway.

State Representative Harry Payne of New Hanover County

State Representative Tom Rabon of Brunswick County

State Representative Tommy Rhodes of New Hanover County

We had two strong allies on the Joint Appropriations Committee, Rep. Harry E. Payne Jr. of New Hanover County and Rep. Tom Rabon Jr. of Brunswick County. Other powerful legislators, including Sen. Bob Jordan, the chairman of the Appropriations Committee and later the state's lieutenant governor, favored that idea, too. Jordan wanted to "maximize" the federal money we could get for our matching state dollars. But many others, including Hunt and his most faithful allies, didn't.

Hunt and his transportation secretary were on record against accepting that ninety-five/five ratio. They didn't want to "tie the hands" of the Board of Transportation (meaning, as a practical matter, Jim Hunt) when it came to allocating highway spending around the state. That meant Hunt was pitting his massive clout against what we were arguing for: An annual commitment of that new federal funding to ensure I-40 wouldn't languish half-built.

By the end of April 1983, things were coming to a head in the legislature. With a vote pending in the joint Appropriations Committee, lobbyists were bending ears and twisting arms. We certainly had an interesting coalition. Republican legislators, led by New Hanover County's Rep. S. Thomas Rhodes, were now on our side. How much some of them sympathized with our need for a better highway, versus how much they simply hoped to thwart Jim Hunt, was hard to tell. Either way, they were useful allies. Also, as Tommy Rhodes said at the time, "We have the Cape Fear Caucus with us, and several members of the Black Caucus have said they'll try to help."

It wouldn't be enough.

A few hours before the committee voted, Hunt distributed to legislators copies of a letter he had written to the editors of the *Morning Star.* He accused the newspaper of selfishness, trying to get "practically all" of the new federal money for I-40. Hunt and his supporters were playing hardball. Their next maneuver was blatant.

Rep. Harry Payne was pushing our position in the General Assembly. He had been promised a chance to speak when the Appropriations Committee met on April 29. His position, Payne recalled recently, was that "We had to minimize the state portion to maximize the federal portion," saving the state millions in addition to keeping our freeway on schedule. But that morning, he was approached by Rep. Allen Adams, a Raleigh Democrat who was one of Hunt's chief legislative allies, and was scheduled to chair that day's committee meeting. Adams was blunt: Payne wouldn't be allowed to speak. Payne's funding proposal, Adams asserted, was "out of order."

While Adams piously assured the hundred-member committee that this was simply a routine procedural matter, the reality is that he didn't want a vote taken. It was a vote he very likely would have lost.

"I'm trying to be a good boy and not let my temper get to me," Payne said that day. "I think they thought it was very close. I don't think they would have done this if they thought we would have lost it."

'Some Little Road to New Hanover County'

While Payne, Rhodes and Rabon were trying to regroup, Adams couldn't resist rubbing salt into the wound. First, he said Payne wouldn't get another chance to bring the matter up until June, at least another month away. Then, when questioned by reporters about his maneuver, he angrily denied that he'd acted under Hunt's orders, or that he'd carried out "any little maneuver at all."

Then came the remark that infuriated and galvanized just about everybody in our corner of the state. "The problem," Adams insisted, was that the state might not have enough money to match the federal dollars, ignoring the reality that our proposal would have saved almost $7 million in state tax revenue over what he and Hunt wanted. "That's a lot more important than whether we have some little road to New Hanover County."

"*Some little road* to New Hanover County." Those words would come back to haunt Al Adams, and indeed Jim Hunt, too.

Rabon predicted as much just hours later. "The next day, those chairs in the audience will be full and these legislators will be hearing about this.

Wilmington Morning Star

Established in 1867 / Vol. 116, No. 171 / Price twenty-five cents / Wilmington, N.C. — Saturday, April 30, 1983

'The problem we're having is that if there isn't enough state money to match the federal money, we may have to make it up with new highway taxes. That's a lot more important than whether we have some little road to New Hanover County.'
Rep. Allen Adams, D-Wake

'I think they thought (the vote on the funds for the road) was very close. I don't think they would have done this (the ruling to cut off debate) if they thought we would have lost it.'
Rep. Harry E. Payne Jr., D-New Hanover

Link to I-40 hits roadblock

Governor opposes grant plan

By Bernadette Hearne
Staff Writer

RALEIGH — Area legislators were thwarted in their attempts to gu funding for the Inter-

In 1983, State Representative Al Adams, one of Governor Hunt's chief allies in the legislature, infuriated I-40 backers by first refusing to let our representative Harry Payne speak, and then by his dismissive remark about 'some little road to New Hanover County.'

When it comes time to vote again, they won't be able to have a voice vote; they'll have to raise their hands."

To that, Payne added, "And that will get blood on their hands, and they don't want that."

Tommy Rhodes was even harsher, laying the whole debacle in Hunt's lap. "He wants to spread the money around outside our area. He thinks Jesse Helms has alienated the people in Southeastern North Carolina so much that he doesn't have to worry about their votes." Rhodes concluded, "I'll make sure the people know what he did to us if we lose this one."

Also making sure the people knew what Hunt did to us was the *Morning Star*'s editorial page. On April 30, right next to Hunt's letter to the editor, the lead editorial was headlined "Hunt betrays our region." Written by Editorial Page Editor Charles Riesz, Jr., the piece accused Hunt of scuttling the I-40 funding "because the deal might put a crimp in his political plans." It went on to say Hunt's "letter was inaccurate." Contrary to the governor's assertion that our deal would eat up "practically all" of the new federal money, the editorial said I-40 would get "only sixteen percent of the increase."

The editorial acknowledged that, as Hunt's letter also said, the governor had helped push I-40 in previous years, and he "deserves credit for that." But then it accused him of choosing "to squander $14 million of the state's money so he can have the flexibility to spend a little money all over the state for political purposes, instead of giving a major boost to an absurdly overdue highway that would benefit the entire state." It concluded with these ominous words: "Hunt deserves credit for that, too. And he can be sure he is going to get it."

Like our legislators and the newspaper, our NC I-40, Inc. wasn't going to take this lying down, either. In fact, we concluded that Hunt's and Adams's ham-handed power play could work to our advantage. "We will have more time to drum up support," I was quoted in the May 1 *Morning Star*. "They might be sorry they didn't try and vote it down. The next time it comes up for a vote there will be a heck of a lot more people in that room."

In retrospect, I suspect that Adams probably wanted to spend the money elsewhere, under the principle that "all roads are political." But I think his dismissive crack also represented the historic lack of recognition and respect that the Raleigh political establishment has always shown to Wilmington and New Hanover County.

Getting our little road built did not entirely stop that prejudice. But it made a big difference.

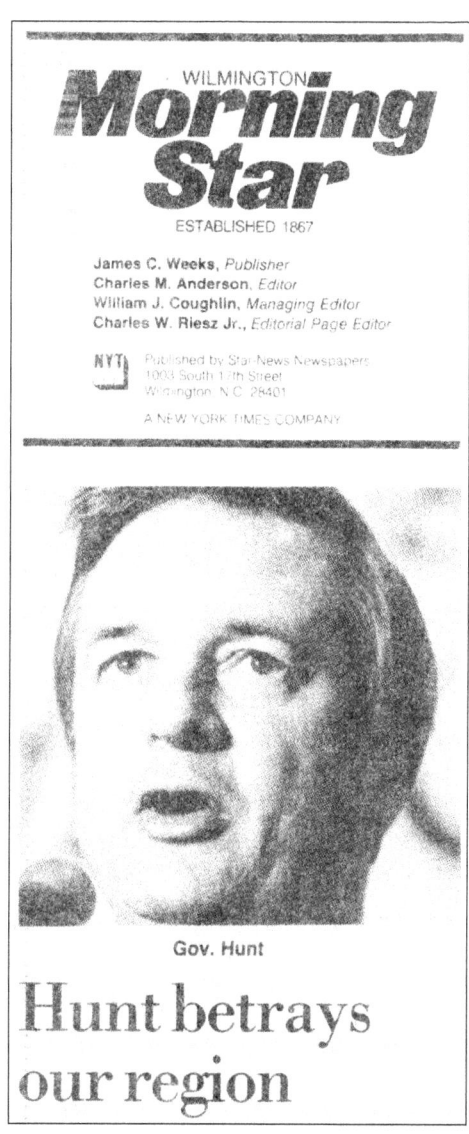

The 'Morning Star' editorial page came out swinging after Jim Hunt's State Board of Transportation shifted federal money away from the I-40 extension, which would have delayed its completion by four years.

* * *

While we were urging I-40 supporters "to get off their you-know-whats" and do whatever they could to influence people in Raleigh, I was also preparing a direct counter to Al Adams about our little road. My time working for the State Ports Authority had helped me understand our port's importance across the state. I compiled a list of companies statewide that shipped through the Wilmington port. I sent it to Adams, for his information, of course. But also to make a broader point with the public: That this was important to the entire state, not just to Wilmington. It wasn't just "some little road."

Tom Rabon showed that our side could play hardball, too. In an April 30 speech to New Hanover County Democrats, he said voters in our corner of the state shouldn't support any candidate for state-wide office who wasn't helping to get I-40 finished.

Back in Wilmington after his confrontation with Al Adams, Harry Payne said he couldn't walk down the street without someone talking with him about the highway. The "spotlight" the "little road" fiasco had put on our project amounted to "the best of all possible worlds" in political terms, he said.

But in Raleigh, he recalled recently, his push for better funding was dead—at least for the 1983 legislative session.

Even so, Payne didn't entirely quit. One day, he rose on the House floor to offer an amendment to change the state's official designation for the I-40 extension. Instead of "X-3," he proposed calling it the "Ramsey-Watkins-Adams Freeway." As he recalled the incident, "That's when Al got mad and jumped up." Payne's tongue-in-cheek suggestion was a dig at House Speaker Liston Ramsey; at Rep. Billy Watkins, who was known as Ramsey's enforcer; and at Al Adams himself. Significantly, Watkins and Adams each chaired one of the House's two appropriations committees. But political theater gets you only so far, and that stunt didn't get us the funding we needed.

During the rest of 1983, the construction contracts already funded did inch forward. That included the beginning of work on another eight miles, stretching northward into Duplin County but still less than halfway to Raleigh.

By year's end, however, little had changed. Hunt and his Board of Transportation remained adamant that only a small fraction of the available funds, just $12.7 million for the 1983-84 budget year, should go toward I-40's extension. They agreed to fund just another eleven miles of construction in 1984, a far slower pace than what they had once promised.

Payne observed then that Hunt might honestly have said, "'The money is there but we've decided $12.7 million is the fair share,'" but chose to assert, falsely, that there wasn't enough money. "To say the pond is dry, when we can see the bass out there jumping," Payne said, "only heightens our feelings and, if I can belabor a metaphor, makes us thirsty."

Did Jim Hunt getting "credit," as that harsh newspaper editorial put it, for his maneuvers around I-40 funding make the difference in the 1984 Senate election? For that matter, did Jesse Helms' die-hard opposition to I-40 on any terms? It's hard to say for sure. Here's how my brother John put it at the end of 1983: "This road is a hell of a lot more important than politics. There are no permanent friends, only permanent causes. This road is our cause."

Among those supporting that cause was Charles "Andy" Anderson, editor of the *Morning Star* and *Sunday Star-News*. In the Christmas Day 1983 edition of his Sunday op-ed column, he poked at Jim Hunt with a parody of the famous 1897 "Yes, Virginia, there is a Santa Claus" essay. Anderson's version was headed, "Yes, Virginia, the highway exists even though you can't drive on it." Ridiculing Hunt for drastically slowing down the project, he concluded, "A thousand years from now, Virginia, nay ten times ten thousand years from now, I-40 will continue to make glad the heart of Southeastern North Carolina. It just won't be finished, that's all. So why didn't you ask us about something real, like Santa Claus?"

That same day, the Sunday newspaper published a feature in which state legislators and

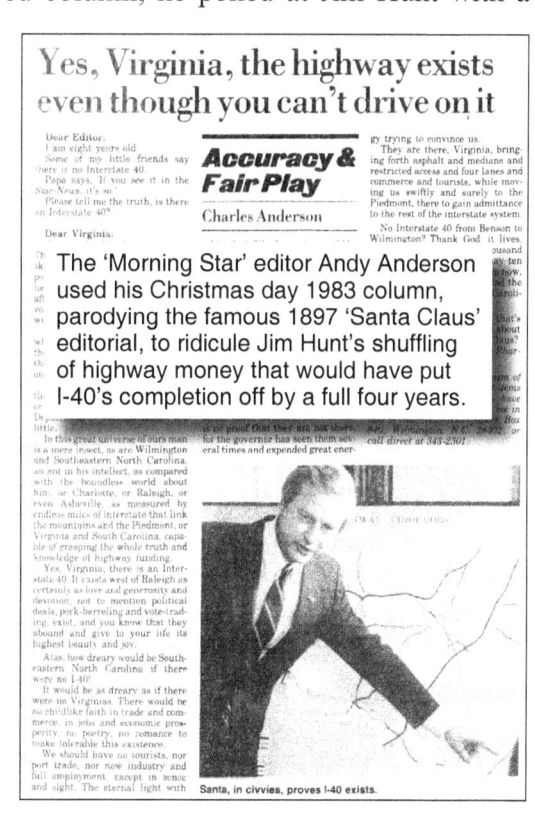

The 'Morning Star' editor Andy Anderson used his Christmas day 1983 column, parodying the famous 1897 'Santa Claus' editorial, to ridicule Jim Hunt's shuffling of highway money that would have put I-40's completion off by a full four years.

> **Say, stranger, how do you get from here to Raleigh?**
>
> For decades, Cape Fear citizens have been grumbling about the bumpy, congested road to Raleigh. The battle for an interstate-style road connecting the port and the Piedmont continues, but in the meantime, many people brave the Wilmington to Raleigh drive on existing two-lane roads.
>
> Among those who drive it on a regular basis, for business or pleasure,
>
> Well, there's 421 to 701 to 55 to 50...
> ... or 421 to 701 to 301 to 70...
> ... or 421 to 242 to 50 to 70...
> ... and then there's the mule train.

A year-end newspaper feature about the convoluted routes necessary to get to the state capital in those pre-I-40 days quoted the author and his father, among others, with cracks about 'mule trains' and 'hogs.' Public and media pressure on Gov. Hunt was building.

other regular travelers offered their opinions about the best way to get to Raleigh. Among those interviewed were my father, who had made that trip many times while serving in the state House of Representatives. Also featured was me. I recommended the variation that went through Newton Grove and on to Raleigh via N.C. 55 and N.C. 50; my father preferred to go the straighter 421-to-701 route.

When the reporter interviewed me, I let my frustration show. Here's how the paper quoted me: "Take a city of Wilmington bus to the city limits, then get a four-wheel drive vehicle to take to Wallace, get yourself a mule train from Wallace to Smithfield, and then walk on from Smithfield to Raleigh." The "mule train" crack made it into the headline.

My father had a similar message, but in fewer words: "I hope before I die I can drive to Raleigh without stopping for a stop sign. Or a hog."

By the end of 1983, he had to have been wishing for at least a dozen more years on this planet. That's because in mid-November we had all learned the grim truth about the Hunt administration's revised construction schedule. It offered a trickle of money each year, stretching the project out to a full ten years. That would have drastically pushed I-40's completion back, all the way to 1994.

It was Andy Anderson's decision to run that front-page story under a monstrous headline, in which nothing but the year "1994," in two-inch-high characters, appeared. A small text block next to the head went on to say, "Southeastern North Carolina's hopes for rapid completion of I-40 to Wilmington were jolted again Friday when the N.C. Department of Transportation allotted only $12.7 million for 1984 construction and set a 10-year construction schedule." In short: that was how long Hunt intended for us to wait for our freeway.

That story quoted my father: "The difference in expectations and realities is a big difference. I lay that at the feet of the governor. The people

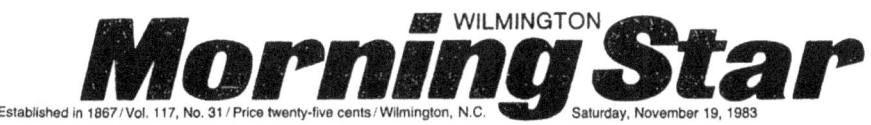

1994: Southeastern North Carolina's hopes for rapid completion of I-40 to Wilmington were jolted again Friday when the N.C. Department of Transportation allotted only $12.7 million for 1984 construction and set a 10-year construction schedule.

Huge headline from November 1983 emphasized that the Wilmington area would have to wait a full eleven years before the freeway would be completed.

in Southeastern North Carolina have been led to believe it would be built faster than this. The governor has let us down."

A New Governor Keeps His Promise

For whatever combination of reasons, Jim Hunt lost the Senate election to Jesse Helms. He would be out of government for the next eight years.

But the 1984 election proved crucial to finally getting the freeway back on track. With Hunt's second term coming to an end, a fresh field of Democrats had vied to replace him in the Governor's Mansion.

The author's father, former State Representative Eugene W. Merritt Senior.

Earlier that year, one of those Democratic primary candidates, Charlotte Mayor Eddie Knox, had asked Harry Payne to draft a position paper on the I-40 extension. Knox prefaced this request with a warning, Payne recalled: "Don't tell the people in Wilmington that they'll get their fair share of the state's highway money." Both Knox and Payne well understood the political realities in Raleigh, at least as they were at the time.

But the political climate was changing. By late 1984, our agitation had succeeded in making the I-40-to-Wilmington project a real issue in

Rufus Edmisten's indifference to the I-40 issue cost him support, and a newspaper endorsement, in the state's southeastern corner.

Running for governor in 1984, Jim Martin promised to get I-40 fully funded during his first term. He kept that promise; it opened in 1990.

the governor's race. In September, the Associated Press wrote a piece about it. The editor of the *Charlotte Observer* wrote a column. And the candidates to replace Hunt as governor were weighing in on the subject. State Attorney General Rufus Edmisten, who had won the Democratic primary, said he would get the freeway finished in six years, but not at the expense of any other highway project. The AP story also quoted him as saying I-40 "is not a burning issue in the state of North Carolina."

Congressman Jim Martin of Charlotte, the Republican candidate, took a sharply different position. He promised that he would divert money from other projects, if necessary, to ensure that all construction contracts to finish I-40 would be signed before his four-year term ended. Harry Payne remembers being impressed that Martin said this not just in Wilmington, but while campaigning in other parts of the state, too.

Martin's promise wasn't the only reason, of course. But it was one major reason why the *Star* endorsed him for governor. It undoubtedly contributed to his victory over Edmisten, who didn't get around to making a strong, direct commitment until just before the election. The endorsement editorial declared plainly, "I-40 is the most important issue facing this part of the state and its economic future."

That seemed to have gotten Jim Hunt's attention. Possibly to help get a fellow Democrat elected to succeed him, Hunt decided in September 1984 to allocate another $16.7 million for I-40. That money had turned up when the rules for federal Interstate Highway funding were changed. And that, in turn, allowed the Hunt administration to back off from his 1994 timeline and again promise the freeway's completion by 1990 or 1991.

In late December 1984, just days before his second term ended, Jim Hunt took a helicopter ride. He flew down to Rocky Point in Pender County, just twenty miles from Wilmington. His mission was to cut a ribbon and open our long-awaited freeway's first eighteen-mile stretch. This ran north from the N.C. 210 interchange and past the new Burgaw exit, concluding for the foreseeable future where I-40 crossed U.S. 117 just south of Wallace. The leg from Wilmington to Rocky Point would take another year to finish because it included major bridges across the Northeast Cape Fear River near Castle Hayne.

After cutting the ribbon and before getting into a waiting car, Hunt told the crowd of some 150 officials and reporters that he would begin his return trip to Raleigh as I-40's first user, before the freeway was actually open to the public. "It's going to be open to me in about fifteen minutes," he said. He likened the new highway to "an early Christmas present. As a matter of fact, it may be the only one I get."

Charlie Rose, who attended the ribbon-cutting, couldn't resist getting in a little dig at Hunt. He said the poet Robert Frost must have had I-40 in mind when he wrote, "I have promises to keep, and miles to go before I sleep."

Hunt concluded the event by saying he had taken so much grief for that highway that he was determined to ride on as much of it as he could while still governor. And so he did.

About to leave office in December 1984, Gov. Jim Hunt opens the first stretch of I-40 in Pender County. After all the grief he had gotten about that highway, he implied at the time, he was determined to ride on it while still governor.

But within a week, regular travelers were using it. And thanks to our new Governor Martin having kept his promises, by 1988 all contracts had been awarded. The entire stretch from Wilmington to Benson opened in the summer of 1990—a good four years sooner than if Hunt had gotten his way.

It's worth noting, by the way, that the freeway was a great deal, financially, for the state. The last ninety miles of I-40 got built at a bargain price: $2.5 million a mile, as of 1983, compared to the state's 1980 average for freeways of $4.3 million per mile. Our region's flat terrain and low rural land values both worked in our favor, keeping right-of-way, engineering and construction costs modest.

And it was no coincidence that, despite all the highway's starts and stops, major investments in tourism and real-estate development were under way in Wilmington by the mid-1980s. That included several hotels and shopping centers near College Road and Market Street, where I-40 traffic would enter the city, and the huge complex of neighborhoods, golf courses, shopping centers and a hotel that would be called Landfall.

* * *

There's no question that I-40 transformed Wilmington's economy. Put another way: Ending Wilmington's isolation, which was a chronic problem for at least two centuries, finally let our sleepy little city become the vibrant community it is now.

A 1999 UNC-Wilmington master's thesis elaborated on this. Its author was Andrew E. Duppstadt, who now runs the education programs for North Carolina's state historic sites. His thesis concerned economic-development efforts in the late Twentieth Century, specifically by what's now called Wilmington Business Development. That organization began in the 1950s under the name "Committee of 100." Duppstadt observed, ". . . by the mid-1970s industrial growth had slowed. In the early 1980s there was another period of substantial growth immediately preceding the area's evolution into a service-based economy." That was largely encouraged, he argued, by gradually improving road access.

For context, he outlined in some detail just how inadequate our region's roads had always been. Throughout the Nineteenth Century, he said, "woefully inadequate" roads were a drag on Wilmington's growth as a seaport. He cited "largely insufficient ground transportation," calling it "a problem that would affect the region's economy and trade well into the Twentieth Century."

By the mid-1950s, when the ACL railroad announced it was pulling its headquarters out of Wilmington, "The Committee of 100 faced the same problems with transportation as previous generations had." And while members of that newly created industrial-recruiting organization knew how poor our highways were, ". . . there is little evidence that they attempted to do much to rectify the situation."

It wasn't just industry that was slow to come. "Tourism was slow to develop," Duppstadt wrote. "This was mainly due to the poor roads and air transportation into the area." Specifically, he said, "It was faster and easier for people in the Charlotte area to go to Myrtle Beach, and the Raleigh area vacationers could get to Morehead City and the surrounding beaches with greater ease."

In his research, the author interviewed my DARE colleague, the banker Rick Willetts. About conditions in the 1960s, Willetts offered this observation: "The saying back then was that you couldn't get to Wilmington by land."

One important metric of a region's economic health is the unemployment rate. For Wilmington, that figure was 3.5 percent in 1970, Duppstadt wrote, "but it rose steadily throughout the 1970s and peaked in 1983 at 11.7 percent." By the mid-1980s, though, the jobless rate had begun to fall. That was partly due to some new industry, and partly to increased tourism. Some of that growth in tourism in the '80s resulted from approval of liquor by the drink, as I've described earlier. Also, by 1988, service businesses had become the area economy's second largest sector, behind wholesale and retail trade. That trend, Duppstadt said, was fueled by population growth, by our community college, university and hospital, and by improved transportation.

"In 1990, when Interstate 40 was finally completed, Wilmington experienced a burst of optimism. The much-awaited major road connection was finally in place. It would bring even more tourists into the area, and would also aid in industrial development."

The sorts of businesses the Committee of 100 was recruiting in the 1990s, Duppstadt wrote, "relied more on faster on-time delivery and better communications, and relied less on the slower types of transportation such as the port."

A few figures—these are from the Southeastern Network for Economic Development Strategy Council, which met in Wilmington in 1991—help tell the story. By 1990, New Hanover County's unemployment rate had fallen to 4.2 percent. That year, the number of service jobs, 17,710, was nearly double the number of jobs in manufacturing.

It wasn't just Wilmington that was benefitting from I-40. Farther north, my father's stomping grounds in Duplin County were also anticipating new business and industrial activity along the freeway's projected route. The Murphy family, hog-farming barons and power players in state politics, would develop their River Landing residential and golf-course complex outside Wallace, a stone's throw from an Interstate exit. In Pender County, a new industrial park was carved out right at the freeway's Burgaw exit.

More recently, a *StarNews* feature about the thirty-fifth anniversary of the freeway's completion noted that New Hanover County's population has more than doubled since 1990. That story cited a few other significant stats for the county: In just the first five years after I-40 opened, single-family housing starts doubled. In that same period, employment growth also more than doubled, from 2.5 percent to 5.5 percent. In the 1990s, tourism spending in the county grew by 52 percent over the previous decade. Was that all due to the freeway? No, not entirely. But there's no doubt that I-40 was by far the most important factor.

But I'm getting ahead of myself again.

At the end of 1984, my father and I concluded that N.C. I-40 Inc. had accomplished its purpose: To make the highway a political issue and to win elected officials' promises to complete it. That was why we decided, shortly after Jim Martin's election, that we could safely disband our organization. We felt that we were able to turn over the leadership on this cause to the political entities. The sales job, both to leaders and the public, had been done.

Right after Thanksgiving in 1984, a *Morning Star* editorial gave my father and me a huge compliment. It began, "'I-40, Inc.' has been dissolved, but the busybody Merritts who started it are still around, thank heaven. Wilmington needs more people like them." It went on to describe our carefully crafted corporation as a "legal fiction," by which the editorial writer meant, "In reality, it was Gene Merritt Sr. and Gene Merritt Jr. butting in where they weren't invited." The editorial said most of the Democratic Party's establishment and the Chamber of Commerce "preferred to be nice to the governor and beg him politely to fulfill his promises." Our supposedly "renegade action" might offend him! But, according to the editorial, we didn't seem to care. Unlike some Democratic big-wigs, it said, we "cared more about Wilmington than about Jim Hunt."

The editorial generously noted that while we couldn't "take all the credit" for getting I-40 finished, we "certainly can take some."

The piece went on to remind readers of the big fight against the proposed downtown coal pile a few years earlier. But that's another story, which I've told in an earlier chapter.

Here, I need to turn some of the *Morning Star*'s complimentary language back in the newspaper's direction. From the very different, fragmented media landscape we inhabit today, it can be hard to appreciate how important a daily newspaper could be in those days. From close coverage by a series of reporters to strong editorial support, most notably from Chuck Riesz and Andy Anderson, the *Morning Star* and *Sunday Star-News* were among our most important allies in getting the highway built.

My brother put it bluntly. "Billy Rose and the *Star-News* were the heroes of this project," he said recently. The paper's coverage and editorials "changed the trajectory," John said, and "helped unbelievably" in mobilizing local support and changing minds in the federal and state governments.

* * *

It was Governor Martin who came to Wilmington on Dec. 20, 1985, to open the essential twelve-mile segment that brought I-40 to the city limits. That now opened thirty miles of the freeway, from here to just south of Wallace, while work continued on its middle third through Duplin and Sampson Counties. Another five miles of that stretch would open in November 1986.

By the time the last ribbons were cut on those last portions linking I-40 with I-95 and Raleigh, Wilmington's South College Road had been transformed. The formerly tree-lined street that funneled traffic from the freeway into town now passed between newly developed shopping centers and gave easy access to brand-new residential subdivisions.

A study of the new highway's economic impact was under way at the time. It was conducted by a business-research arm of UNC-Charlotte, with help from state agencies and local governments along the right of way. It predicted that I-40 would help boost job growth in the highway corridor by thirty-five percent during the next twenty years. As it turned out, in the twenty years after July 1990, the five counties along I-40 between Wilmington and I-95 saw fifty percent job growth!

Town & Country

WILMINGTON
Morning Star

Established in 1867 / Vol. 123, No. 222 / Price twenty-five cents / Wilmington, N.C.   Saturday, June 30, 1990

It's open!

With snip of ribbon, I-40 opens

By Janet Olson
Staff Writer

NEWTON GROVE — About 3,000 people christened the final stretch of Interstate 40 Friday with streams of sweat.

They traveled on two-lane highways from miles around to gather here at the N.C. 50-55 overpass, where they stood on a section of fresh black asphalt and wilted under a blazing sun.

They endured the heat for one reason: to see it for themselves. Interstate 40 between Raleigh and Wilmington is no longer a dream.

As the day approached high noon, a beaming Gov. Jim Martin delivered on the only highway promise he ever made to voters.

"When I ran for governor in 1984, I made just one highway campaign promise," Martin said. "That was to get Interstate 40 between Raleigh and Wilmington under contract by the end of my first term. I made good on that in 3½ years.

"... I asked you to believe that I

Please see I-40, 9A

Before a huge crowd of spectators, dignitaries cut the ribbon Friday in Newton Grove to open the last leg of interstate 40.

3,000 turn out to celebrate interstate's opening

■ U.S. 17, U.S. 74 widenings, 1C
■ More photos from I-40, 3C

By Merton Vance
Regional Editor

NEWTON GROVE — While others celebrated the completion of Interstate 40 on Friday with speeches, bands, singing and airplane flyovers, some marked the occasion with produce.

Underneath the N.C. 50 overpass across I-40 sat 500 white paper bags, each printed with a message calling Sampson County "The Last Link" in the interstate.

Each bag bore samples of locally grown cantaloupes, tomatoes, peppers, cucumbers, eggplants and sweet potatoes.

"If we'd known this was going to bring this big of a crowd, we'd have had a tobacco leaf or two and maybe a hog stuck in 'em," said George

unofficial barbecue-sandwich-and-hot-dog-method of crowd estimating: Eddie's Cafe in Newton Grove catered 2,600 barbecue sandwiches and 900 hot dogs, and by the time

Others gathered in the shade under the overpass, where there was a breeze, but a generator drowned out the speakers — a disadvantage or an advantage, depending on one's point of view.

A caravan moves eastward on I-40 from Newton Grove to Warsaw.

Gov. Jim Martin; Barstow, Calif., Mayor Bill Pope; Wilmington Mayor Don Betz and Raleigh Mayor Avery Upchurch unveil a road

After more than a dozen years of effort, the freeway's completion was big news in 1990.

Among the heroes of the fight to get I-40 funded and built: Congressman Charlie Rose with his chief of staff, John Merritt, the author's brother. More than once, Rose called in favors to get federal funding directed specifically to the freeway extension between I-95 and Wilmington.

It was a blisteringly hot day in June 1990 when our freeway's last segment was opened, between northern Duplin County and the I-95 interchange. The ceremony was held near Newton Grove, where a patch of colorful petunias, planted to form an outline of a North Carolina map, wilted in the heat as dignitaries—including Gov. Jim Martin—orated.

I didn't go.

All the politicians were posturing and taking credit for the road. I felt that my work had been done, and that I had no need to hog credit for it. Already by then, my father and I had received ample recognition for our work, both for I-40 and against the downtown coal pile. The ceremony at Newton Grove was full of politicians busy patting themselves on their own backs.

I didn't care. I knew what we had done: The dirty work.

5. Other Windmills to Tilt at

I'm not young anymore. Many of the most important battles I've described took place decades ago. But somehow, the instinct to see problems that need solving, and the urge to do something about them, has never left me. So instead of resting on my laurels and easing into a dignified retirement, I seem to be always finding a new cause to take on.

These might not have been as consequential as getting our city linked by freeway to the rest of the world. But they were still important. And even these smaller, latter-day battles carry lessons for other Citizen Warriors to learn from.

Creating the River-to-Sea Rotary Run

This first project actually came before I even went to work at DARE. When I returned to Wilmington in the 1970s, I followed my father's example and joined the Wilmington Rotary Club.

As a young Rotarian, I found myself focused on creating something new. The objective was to promote physical fitness and cardiac health through exercise. The result was what we called the Rotary Run. In its first year, it was also a fund-raiser for the club. Eventually it would be fully adopted by the Wilmington Road Runners club, which now calls it the River-to-the-Sea run.

That first year, I ended up chairing the committee that got it started.

To make it appealing to as many people as possible, we divided the event into four simultaneous runs, all ending at Wrightsville Beach. The original river-to-the-sea course—we billed it as "the Heartbreaker"—started in downtown Wilmington. The other three options were shorter, to allow runners at every level to participate. More than 600 people signed up to run, and more than 550 of them finished.

In the lead-up to the May 8, 1978 road race, our committee preached the gospel of fitness and heart health to our fellow Rotarians. At one meeting, a month before the race, we enlisted two experts from the YMCA to help with a dramatic demonstration of how to prepare for serious exertion while defending against cardiovascular disease. Our fitness-expert guests needed a guinea pig. I volunteered.

The YMCA visitors demonstrated how they offered an EKG stress testing program to determine "present ability to take, do, or perform exercise," and to recommend an appropriate exercise program for the client, the club newsletter recounted. It went on to say, "A 'volunteer' (Gene Merritt, Jr.) stepped forward, stripped to the waist, had the EKG wires attached, stepped on the treadmill, and then proceeded to demonstrate . . . the way the test is given and information recorded." That report concluded, "The Rotary Run is trying to call the attention of everyone to this bit of advice: Exercise (intelligently) for your life."

That was the only time a public cause required me to bare quite so much of myself physically. But it set a precedent: Sometimes, you just need to be willing to set an example for your intended audience.

Extending Revitalization up North Fourth Street

During my time at DARE, I was regularly urged to pay attention to a once-thriving business street that, by the 1970s and '80s, had become badly neglected. Earlier, during the worst days of Jim Crow, North Fourth Street was a vital hub for African-Americans: A place where they could shop, dine, listen to music, and go to the movies without suffering the humiliations and insults that were common for Black patrons in White-owned businesses. But as segregation came to an end, and Black customers became welcomed in the mainstream retail community, North Fourth Street's businesses languished.

By the 1970s, that once bustling strip was suffering from the same ills as Wilmington's main business district. Also a drag on business were low incomes and deterioration in the surrounding residential neighborhoods, known as Brooklyn and the Northside.

Eventually, the handful of remaining merchants on North Fourth decided it was past time to do something about this.

One of them was Harry Forden. He ran a store, the Fourth Street Bargain House, and was a long-time political leader in Wilmington's Precinct One. He was also the guiding spirit behind the North Fourth Street Partnership in 1992. With Forden's encouragement, I was its co-founder and served on its board. In 1993, Wilmington's City Council allocated $213,000 in federal grant funds to the Partnership. In addition to creating a revolving loan fund for business start-ups and improvements, like DARE had begun in the 1970s, this would help cover operating funds. That allowed the Partnership to hire a staff.

At the end of the year, Forden approached me about working as the group's part-time executive director. They wanted the benefit of my experience in the Central Business District. I really hadn't planned on this, but as a news report at the time quoted me, "I was looking for a challenge, and this will be one." Just like at DARE, I concluded, I would need help from a promotion director and a secretary, both part-time.

At the start, I decided that it was important to make a symbolic gesture: I put my downtown building, where my real estate company had its office, on the market, and started looking for an address on North Fourth.

Among my immediate plans were to work with the people who established the New Hanover Community Health Center, the community clinic now known as MedNorth Health Center, and to help businesses along North Fourth Street to get financing. Over the next couple of years, we were able to recruit several new businesses and see the health clinic getting ready to open.

But by early 1996, I realized I had to back away from that job. It was hard to do two things at one time. I'd had a mild heart attack the summer before, and worries about my health and my own business meant I couldn't devote the time or energy that the job required. But we had made a good start.

Even though I spent only a couple of years in the job, I am proud of what we accomplished. Today, that formerly neglected commercial strip is called the Brooklyn Arts District. Its anchor is the former St. Andrews Church building, which is now a popular event space called the Brooklyn

Arts Center. Even after leaving the Partnership, I stayed involved with that project. I served for a time in the early 2000s as president of the non-profit that stabilized the badly deteriorated building and sold it to the developers who finished its restoration.

The Brooklyn Arts District boasts multiple eating and drinking places, new residential buildings, retail shops, and the city's main downtown transit hub. In 2025, it became New Hanover County's first "social district," where pedestrians are permitted to carry and drink alcoholic beverages on the street on Saturday afternoons. That has become yet another attraction for visitors. I believe the North Fourth Street Partnership was the foundation of today's success in that neighborhood.

Saving Waterfront Dining in North Carolina

In the late 1990s, I got interested in the landmark J.W. Brooks Grocery building on Water Street. Its last tenant had been the offices of the Stone Towing Company, whose tugboats had been moored nearby as late as the early 1980s. But though it had been empty for years, the building had what we call "good bones." Dating from 1920, it had been solidly built; its architect, William J. Wilkins, also designed New Hanover High School's original 1922 building. It presented a perfect opportunity to convert a sturdy old warehouse for commercial and residential use.

And because it sits right along the Cape Fear River, I saw another perfect opportunity: To extend the Riverwalk. In 1988, the city had enlarged the Riverfront Park that began with our UDAG project six years earlier. In addition to building a long-needed visitor center, public restrooms, and a covered picnic area, that project brought the Riverwalk 160 feet south of Market Street, right up to the Brooks Building. But there it stopped.

In 1995, I went into a partnership with Gene Strader, whose expertise lay in both commercial real estate and the marina business. We planned to build a marina next to the extension of that public walkway alongside the old Brooks Building. But soon, we discovered a serious obstacle. I was told that state environmental regulations prohibited building a structure over "public trust waters" for any purpose that wasn't "water-dependent." Those public waters most definitely included the navigable Cape Fear River.

So our marina could have been permitted, because a marina is water-dependent. But a scenic, recreational public promenade like the Riverwalk could not. As riverfront restaurants already knew, of course, you could also forget about serving food or drinks on any structure over those public waters.

Those regulations had been issued by the state Coastal Resources Commission. The CRC was created in 1974 to enforce the new Coastal Area Management Act. Both CAMA and the CRC were considered national leaders in environmental protection. They did a lot to protect North Carolina's coast. But they weren't perfect. These regs were a perfect example.

By the 1990s, waterfront dining was a major draw in Wilmington, bringing both tourists and locals downtown. It had been pioneered, in the late 1970s, in Thomas Wright's Chandler's Wharf. There, The Pilot House restaurant became Wilmington's very first dining establishment with a river view. Soon after that, one of the high-profile projects I had worked on during my time at DARE, the Fish Market Restaurant, opened just diagonally across Water Street from the Brooks Grocery building. Its owner had added balconies overlooking the river, which became a major draw for couples looking for a romantic dining experience. The success of those downtown pioneers had encouraged other restaurateurs to offer riverview dining areas.

But now, these state rules were preventing the Pilot House's owners, who also operated Elijah's Restaurant right next door, from extending their popular decks past the high tide mark. The same rules effectively blocked the city government from extending the Riverwalk south of Market Street, because it would have to be built over water. (Those restrictions hadn't affected the Riverwalk's original stretch, between Market and Princess Streets. That had been built on solid ground, behind bulkheads already in place.)

Similar issues hampered other dining spots along the riverfront. Away from downtown, the state rules affected restaurants on the Intracoastal Waterway, in both Wilmington and Wrightsville Beach. Not to mention in North Carolina's dozens of other coastal towns.

So besides being a major drawback in my own plans, this was a serious problem for many other businesses, too. Although I would have done the Brooks Building project with or without the Riverwalk, this seemed like too important an issue to walk away from.

A 2024 CRC historical report about this says the commission's staff first began considering special rules for "Urban Waterfront Areas of Environmental Concern" in 1995. What the study doesn't mention is that this was triggered by pressure from Wilmington: Specifically, from me.

I lobbied the CRC but got no help. The Commission's history says its attention "was sidelined due to a shift in priorities in the aftermath of Hurricanes Bertha and Fran in 1996." Those storms, which hit Wilmington back to back in July and September, were indeed a major distraction for most of us. It would take another year for the CRC to take up the matter again. The agency's history also neglects to mention that it was legislative action on our behalf that spurred it into action.

I had already concluded that we would have to enlist the General Assembly to force the CRC's hand. And so we started communicating with legislators. Not just our own, but those representing other coastal communities, which were facing similar issues. And with support from up and down the coast, and even from some inland cities with developed riverfronts, we managed to get legislative relief.

I found a key ally in State Rep. Thomas Wright—no relation to the Chandler's Wharf developer of the same name. In April 1997, he introduced House Bill 1059. After some back-and-forth between House floor and committees, it passed in April, got the state Senate's approval, and was signed by Gov. Jim Hunt in July.

The bill's gist was to require the CRC to grant permits for certain "urban waterfront redevelopment in historically urban areas." To qualify, a city or town had to meet some common-sense criteria, including a history of urban development or compatible local zoning, and the local government's endorsement of a particular project as "significantly increasing public access." Also, going back to the disputed regulations' original purpose, a project couldn't have a "significant adverse impact on the environment."

One quirk in the law was that it wasn't permanent. It had been amended to expire July 1, 2000, by which time presumably the CRC would have revised its regulations accordingly.

But it didn't. Instead, the CRC staff seemed determined to revert to the previous situation, and once again bar from waterfronts all but "water-dependent" businesses like marinas. That, of course, would directly harm restaurants with waterfront dining areas.

So well before the 2000 deadline arrived, once again I had to enlist allies. This time, we had to make our case directly to the CRC. An especially vital ally was DARE, where Bob Murphrey was then executive director. In December 1998, he wrote to the CRC's relevant committees, using talking points I had proposed to him.

Popular riverside dining areas, like this deck at Elijah's in Chandler's Wharf, are possible because of a change to state environmental rules. Spurred by legislation and lobbying, the new regulations allowed restaurants and bars to operate over public waters.

"Like many other towns and cities along the North Carolina Coast," Murphrey wrote, "we are very concerned about the negative effect of the Commission's proposed rule changes for shoreline development." A month later, on Jan. 27, 1999, the DARE board adopted a resolution that likewise opposed the CRC's "proposed shoreline regulation changes."

DARE's argument—and mine—boiled down to the "significant differences" between the rural wetlands the CRC was charged with protecting and the urban waterfronts, like ours, that had been used intensively for centuries. Encouraging new uses of the already "densely developed" urban waterfronts, we contended, actually helped meet the CRC's mandate, by reducing the environmental impact of continuing suburban sprawl. Murphrey's letter and the board's resolution both made the same point: What we were doing in Wilmington was converting our riverfront from industrial use to commercial, residential, and recreational, actually mitigating environmental harm.

The CRC's rules required broad buffers between commercial users and public waters. That was out of synch with urban realities. City land is divided into small lots. Most city lots, like those on our waterfront, are too small to meet the CRC's rules on setbacks and maximum lot coverage. DARE's resolution noted that the rules ignored many towns' efforts "to provide public access along our urban waterfronts, allowing the public to enjoy the benefits of the water as well."

DARE asked the CRC to amend its rules to permanently "exempt urban waterfronts from these provisions," as HB 1059 specified.

At this stage, our allies included the late Donna Girardot of the Wilmington Regional Association of Realtors, and local leaders from other waterfront communities. They formed what was called the "N.C. Coastal Coalition." At the end of January, 1999, Long Beach Mayor Joan Altman was scheduled to speak on behalf of that coalition when the CRC met in Kill Devil Hills.

Unfortunately, our proposal—which affected less than one percent of the state's shorelines—was up against a network of fourteen environmental groups led by the N.C. Coastal Federation, which saw any loosening of the CRC's rules as a threat to the genuinely imperiled coastal environment. We didn't want to be their enemies—but we couldn't let arbitrary rules harm businesses that were no threat to the public waters the rules were supposed to protect.

And so when the CRC met in Atlantic Beach on March 23, 2000, a large delegation from Wilmington was there. Bob Murphrey spoke on DARE's behalf.

Urging that HB 1059's provisions become permanent regulations, he repeated many of the arguments he and I had been making. Then he offered what I still take as a personal compliment: "The draft rules you have proposed for urban waterfronts are certainly recognition of these special waterfront areas; recognition that was first pointed out several years ago through the efforts of a Wilmington native, Gene Merritt, Jr., who is here with us today, and other Wilmington citizens and government officials. Their efforts resulted in the passage of state legislation designed to allow non-water dependent uses over public trust waters along urban waterfronts."

Our presentation to the CRC included my comparison of the rules then current and what the CRC had proposed to replace them.

Finally, the CRC relented, a bit. At its May 26, 2000 meeting, it adopted new rules for urban waterfronts. Those followed local zoning, and specified that an "urban waterfront" meant shorelines "where there is minimal undeveloped land, mixed land uses, and urban level services." In these areas, no buffer was required, and other requirements were relaxed.

Most important: To be eligible for food or drink service, any structure over public waters had to be built on pilings. And for reasons nobody ever clearly justified, these over-the-water dining areas had to be not just open-air, but completely exposed to the elements. They couldn't even have a roof. So a bar on an open deck would be fine; a bar in a gazebo, forbidden.

Already, Rep. Wright had introduced another bill, at our request, to extend H.B. 1059 for one year. And as Bob Murphrey put it at the time, CRC was seeking support for its proposed new rules, "hoping to avoid a confrontation."

So were we. Based on "the opinion of those most actively involved in the process to date," Murphrey recommended that we accept the relaxed CRC rules. "New legislation could be developed and entered later if necessary."

We had gotten something more than half a loaf, and I agreed with Murphrey's advice. On June 7, 2000, I wrote to Rep. Wright: "We are in agreement with the CRC and wish to try to work within the rules." I asked him to work with the Coastal Management staff to draft legislation that would put the newest urban waterfront rules "in effect as temporary measures."

And so he was able to slip our extension of H.B. 1059 into a much larger bill, entitled "An act to amend various environmental laws." Along with seven unrelated measures, this new bill nudged our temporary urban-waterfront provisions forward nine months, to April 2001. That quickly passed the state House; the state Senate approved it on July 5, 2000, and Gov. Hunt signed it into law Aug. 2.

Did we get everything we wanted? No. The ban on enclosing waterfront dining areas was a significant drawback to the compromise we worked out with the CRC. But even so, protecting the right to serve food and drink on waterfront decks was a very important accomplishment. It made a big difference in how downtown Wilmington developed in the Twenty-first Century.

Just as important was that this cleared the way for the major extensions of the Riverwalk, both south and north, that have become such a valuable amenity—and tourist attraction—for Wilmington. In January 2025, a *StarNews* story called the Riverwalk Wilmington's "top tourist destination." Four years earlier, a Gannett/*USA Today* poll ranked it the nation's second-best riverwalk, behind only Detroit. Wilmington was the only small city in that poll's top ten, which was dominated by such major metro communities as Philadelphia, San Antonio, Chicago, and Boston.

When the extension of H.B. 1059 expired on April 1, 2001, the CRC adopted the current rule, which largely follows what that law had required. As it stands now, that allows for roofs, but no other enclosures, and for restaurants and retail shops, but no other "non-water-dependent" commercial uses. So a restaurant could get a permit to build a deck with a gazebo, and to serve its customers there.

As I write this, the CRC's staff has proposed an amendment, inspired by a downtown Wilmington restaurant that happens to be right next door to the Brooks Building. If adopted, that new rule would permit non-permanent enclosures such as vinyl curtains, thus allowing outdoor dining areas to be used in cold or rainy weather.

Looking back, I found an essay about our project on the UNC-Wilmington "History Hub" website. It says Gene Strader and I had fundamentally changed how the J.W. Brooks Building could be used, and deserved to be mentioned on its historic-property plaque. It also said, "It is also because of their renovations that there is an extension of the Riverwalk on the water side of the building, meaning the J.W Brooks building is more accessible to get into and around." The piece quotes a remark I had made in a newspaper interview: The Brooks project had "revitalized a part of Wilmington that was once considered 'skid row,' contributing to the city's development and tourism."

Even more important, though: All the agitation that followed also revitalized the restaurant business, not just downtown but everywhere along North Carolina's coast. Just as important: while I might have begun the agitating, it was by building alliances, and balancing public pressure with pragmatic compromises, that this victory was won.

Water Street Center

As I've mentioned in the chapter on DARE, Inc., a large parking deck had dominated Wilmington's downtown waterfront since the mid-1960s. It extended two blocks, from Grace Street almost to Princess. It occupied prime land that, by the middle 1990s, was clearly more valuable for commercial and residential use than it was for parking cars. New parking garages developed by both the city and county governments were providing lots more off-street space for downtown employees and visitors to stash their cars. And liberating the city to wash its hands of the matter, the bonds it had sold to build the thing had finally been paid off.

Starting in 1994, DARE was lobbying a rapidly growing new business, Pharmaceutical Product Development, Inc., to consolidate its downtown offices, putting all 200 of its employees in one building. DARE's plan was to make PPD the anchor tenant in a proposed new office building on the parking deck site. Unfortunately, that deal got scuttled by the City Council, with Councilman Harper Peterson—who would become mayor in 2001—its chief antagonist. His opposition centered on a long and contentious debate about acceptable building heights in the Central Business District.

As councilman and mayor, Harper Peterson was often at odds with the author over development projects in the 1990s and early 2000s.

One side of that argument held that downtown should be largely frozen in its current state, and that tall new buildings would be out of scale with their surroundings. The counter was that Wilmington is a living city, not a museum, and that multi-story buildings are not just appropriate in much of downtown, but necessary.

Regardless of the merits of those arguments, the upshot was that PPD felt distinctly unwelcome downtown. In August 1995, after the city killed its office deal, the company accepted an offer to move its headquarters to a new suburban site, near where the Cameron Art Museum stands now. The loss of those hundreds of corporate employees was a serious blow to downtown, but the damage had been done. It would be a dozen years later, in 2007, before PPD finally returned, building a ten-story headquarters tower at the north end of downtown. Ultimately, in 2023, after a merger, PPD's new owners would sell that building to the city; it now houses most of the city government's offices.

Even after the 1995 PPD debacle, the city staff was still looking for ways to make better use of the parking deck site. It issued a call for proposals on "a mixed-use development of retail, office, and residential spaces" where the deck stood.

And so in 1997 I bid on that project. My $1.5 million bid won. My development company would buy the entire 1966 parking deck and the land beneath it, with plans to quickly demolish the deck's southern third. While developing that tract, my company would keep operating the other two-thirds, collecting hourly and monthly parking fees.

Shortly after that deal was concluded, I was interviewed for a newspaper feature. It quoted me about how I would think my way through a development project: "I sit right here with a lemonade or an iced tea, and I make myself sit and look at the building for two hours. I think the opposite of normal thoughts. And sometimes you get visions."

But despite my visions, and despite the city picking me to redevelop the parking deck site, the sale took another two years to wrap up. The deal didn't close until February 2000.

By then, in partnership with John Sutton, who had recently renovated the huge Masonic Temple building on North Front Street, and Stuart Cooke, also an experienced developer, I had formed Water Street Center Associates LLC. The nine-story Water Street Center, Phase I, to be built on part of the parking deck site, combined retail space at street level with residential condominiums on the upper floors. We finished construction in 2001.

We had other plans for the rest of the site. Those included a new multi-level parking garage to be tucked away behind the original building, and eventually additional mixed-use buildings where the remnant of the old deck stood. In 2002, I reminded Mayor Peterson and the City Council that the city had offered the site "to any developer who would provide a new and attractive development that generated jobs, tax base, and services" and would "provide a needed pedestrian linkage between the Cotton Exchange on the North and Chandler's Wharf on the South."

To fulfill those goals, I proposed two new phases to Water Street Center. Those included reopening the block of Chestnut Street between Front and Water Streets; in 1966 that block had been closed and the street's stub end became the parking deck's vehicle entrance. My proposal also called for extending the park where the long-gone Bijou Theater once stood, and erecting a new building near the center of the parking deck site.

I won't bog down this account by rehashing all the economic and political factors that got in the way. To make a long story short, I never did get to Phases II and III. In 2007, the city bought back the remaining portion of the old parking deck, and eventually re-sold it. Much of what I had proposed, including reopening Chestnut Street, was eventually done by other developers. But it got done! That new complex of multi-story mixed-use buildings, called River Place, has finally restored that site to its full development potential.

Even so, the original Water Street Center remains an important landmark. It was a distinctive addition to the downtown skyline. It brought street-level retail back to North Water Street, and its upper floors became a tourism amenity. Many of the building's residential condominiums are managed as vacation rental properties, bolstering downtown's tourist trade.

Water Street Center, which the author built in the early 2000s, replaced part of the parking deck that the city had erected during the urban renewal era of the 1960s.

Water Street Center wasn't my only private development, but it's the biggest and most visible, and one I'm still proud of. Its history also contains some lessons about the potential, but also the perils and pitfalls, of trying to balance business and politics in a historic community.

Saving 'One Tree Hill'

In May 2003, I was visiting Red's, my favorite bar in downtown Wilmington. I ran into Ron Moncovich, one of my drinking buddies. At the time, Ron represented the Teamsters Union on the set of *One Tree Hill*. That television series had just filmed its pilot in Wilmington and was expected to go into full production soon.

Ron was distressed. He said *One Tree Hill*'s producers had decided to move their operations to Vancouver, British Columbia. It wasn't that they didn't like working in Wilmington, or the various locations around town; the decision was purely financial. At that time, Canada was offering significant financial incentives to attract film productions. As things stood in those days, North Carolina was not competitive with those incentives.

Ron told me that the production leaving Wilmington would have a major economic impact. He, personally, would lose his job. He also said the local film commission's leaders had accepted the fact that the show was leaving. They had done nothing to try to save the production.

This greatly irritated me, being a person who appreciated the film industry's benefits to Wilmington and the southeastern North Carolina region. At that moment, I resolved that I would do anything and everything I could to save the production. I also had my reasons for wanting to stave off Ron's potential unemployment: I did not want to have to buy his drinks in the bar.

At that time, the state of North Carolina did have a modest, newly created film incentive fund. It held a balance of $500,000. I believed we had to try to get all of that money dedicated to *One Tree Hill*. If we could get it, along with some possible local incentive money, we might be able to match or better the Canadian offer. We determined that we needed $750,000.

I knew something had to be done quickly if we were to have any chance of saving this production. Not being in the film industry, I had no contacts there. However, I did have some political connections.

My first step was to call for an emergency meeting with the Wilmington Regional Film Commission. On May 23, 2003, I met with Johnny Griffin, the film commission's director; Frank Capra, Jr. of the EUE-Screen Gems movie studio; my brother John; and State Rep. Danny McComas. We met several times in the next few days. George Rountree III, the president of the film commission, joined us at the second meeting. Rountree, a former

State Representative Danny Mc-Comas took the lead in getting state incentive funds for 'One Tree Hill.'

state legislator and a Republican like McComas, had political connections and clout of his own.

I presented my idea: To ask the state for the full $500,000 from its film-incentive fund and the city and county governments for $125,000 each. That would get us our hoped-for total of $750,000.

By that time, my political-insider brother John was working in Raleigh, where he had developed valuable contacts in state government. He and I were also friends of McComas, who owned a Wilmington trucking company. I decided that the key to getting our hands on the state's half-million dollars would be through the good efforts of John Merritt and Danny McComas. John had valuable connections with legislative Democrats, while McComas could count on relationships with his fellow Republicans. Both were comfortable working across the aisle with members of the other party, too.

They started working on the State Film Commission money.

John had some experience with this. Earlier, working for Governor Mike Easley, he had helped steer some state money in our direction for the final season of the hit series *Dawson's Creek*. At my request, he had met with both Capra, the studio chief, and the head of the state's film program. At the time, the state was leaning toward directing those funds toward a Charlotte movie production. John's persuasion—no doubt influenced by the fact that he had the governor's ear—got the incentive pot reallocated to Wilmington, thus helping *Dawson's Creek* finish its run here.

When this issue came up again with *One Tree Hill*, we still had support from the governor's office. But even though the legislature had recently approved the new film-incentive fund, it took serious lobbying to get the money we needed.

As John recalls it, Danny McComas did most of that lobbying.

After the fact, George Rountree made a point of ensuring that McComas got due credit for securing that those half-million state dollars. A July 20, 2003, *StarNews* story quoted Rountree saying McComas had worked across the aisle to influence Democrats in the state House of Representatives. Rountree also credited John, who had been working as a "senior policy assistant" to Gov. Mike Easley.

The same story quoted John about the importance of McComas's work. "If you want to get into heaven, you've got to be kind to some Republicans."

And so, with help from John, McComas got a commitment from the state for $500,000. That was the entire pot of film-incentive money the legislature had already appropriated. This was a strong echo of the situation with Interstate 40 in 1983 and 1984: Would the lion's share of a state budget line be devoted to a Wilmington-focused project—some little TV show in New Hanover County—or should those dollars be spread around the state in dribs and drabs? In this case, although other places in the state were venturing into the film business, Wilmington stood alone. Our "Hollywood East" nickname was justified, what with the extensive sound stages at the Screen Gems studio on Twenty-third Street and the many skilled professionals who had gravitated to it over the previous twenty years. But as with any political question, pure logic and fairness weren't enough. It took the savvy and personal connections that John and Danny could bring to bear to get that money safely directed our way.

Then there was the matter of the local money.

We decided that Rountree would solicit New Hanover County for $125,000 and I would ask the City of Wilmington for the same amount.

Rountree was able to persuade the County Commissioners to tap a contingency fund that still had money in it near the end of the 2002-03 budget year.

It took a bit more doing to get the City's contribution. As it happened, Harper Peterson, Wilmington's mayor at the time, was out of town just then. At that time, he and I were not getting along very well. I was confident that if I had to go to him directly that he would not help. Fortunately, I was able to get help from City Manager Sterling Cheatham while Harper wasn't around to block it. What Cheatham did was to put the $125,000 in his proposed budget for the upcoming 2003-04 fiscal year.

In late May, Cheatham said he had discussed the matter individually with members of the City Council and that most seemed to support it. Soon afterward, the Council approved the budget, and with it the $125,000 incentive.

McComas emphasized that getting the money for *One Tree Hill* was a one-time deal. Because the state hadn't yet formalized its film-incentive program, the city and county authorities had leeway to set their own conditions. One of those, imposed by the City Council, was that the series would be filmed within the city limits. Fortunately, the Screen Gems studio, as well as most of the locations the show used, met that qualification.

The city's budget got us to our $750,000 target.

The bottom line is that in just three days we raised the money and presented it to the local film commission. With that three quarters of a million in his pocket, Griffin then went to *One Tree Hill*'s producers and matched the Canadian offer. Shortly afterwards, they announced that they would accept our bid. The show would be filmed in Wilmington.

Capra, the studio director, said it was the first time that a city, a county, and a state had teamed up to lure a production. "It's kind of a breakthrough," he was quoted in a May news story. It was also a job creator. At the time, Griffin projected that the show could hire 125 people full-time, plus 3,000 part-time positions. And that was just in its first season.

George Rountree III secured New Hanover County funds to help retain 'One Tree Hill.'

The *One Tree Hill* series filmed for nine years in Wilmington until the show concluded in 2012. During that time, its economic impact on the city and the region was in the hundreds of millions of dollars. The production provided lots of good jobs; it bought many local goods and services. The economic impact far outweighed the public dollars invested in it.

Making the show cost about $20 million per season. Over nine years, that amounted to around $180 million, most of it spent here. Of course, those numbers don't include the total economic impact the production had, with every dollar spent eventually changing hands several more times. They also don't reflect the intangible benefits. A 2012 *StarNews* story about *One Tree Hill* quoted veteran crew members who said the show had made it possible for them to live and raise their families here.

Wilmington City Manager Sterling Cheatham found $125,000 for 'One Tree Hill.'

Hugely popular as *One Tree Hill* was, memories of its production still contribute to Wilmington's tourism industry. Fans come from all over the globe to visit the sites where the show was filmed.

I was very proud to have led the efforts to keep the production in Wilmington.

I think members of the local film commission—and some others closely connected to them—were a bit embarrassed that an outsider would be able to accomplish what they could not. The people officially responsible for promoting Wilmington's film business had accepted the loss of the show when it was poised to move to Canada. I suspect that embarrassment explains why they scarcely acknowledged my contributions.

Regardless of my feelings, though, I believe what we did—raising the money in just a few days and saving what ended up as a nine-year production—was well worth the effort.

Governor's Landing

Late in the Twentieth Century, various investors and developers saw business opportunities along the Cape Fear River. One of them was named David Steigerwald. Doing business as Riverview Properties, he saw the empty land at the foot of Nun Street as a promising spot for a small condominium project. His idea was to build nine townhouses with views of the river.

It seemed like a good idea at the time.

But all development projects are not created equal. And this one began with several strikes against it, including under-capitalization and the developer's questionable skills.

He hadn't made much progress before neighbors started to notice problems.

The April 13, 2000 minutes of the city's Historic Preservation Commission tell part of the story. The commission is responsible for enforcing rules about architectural details in Wilmington's Historic Districts. The most important of those, wrapped around the Central Business District's southern half, includes Nun Street.

During the commission's discussion of architectural details such as doors, gables, and such, a nearby property owner stood up to speak. That neighbor lived on Church Street, at the top of a bluff overlooking the project. She "asked why this is being discussed when Mr. Steigerwald has not followed the plans on file," the commission's minutes say. "His construction practices, from her observations, leave a lot to be desired. He did not follow the special use permit and he didn't protect any trees. They

While completing the Governor's Landing condo project on Nun Street, the author built this extension of the Riverwalk in front of the property before turning it over to the city.

were pulled up with a backhoe, shaken and dumped. He didn't protect the historic wall which was part of the special use permit. He undermined her wall, which was a new wall."

It only got worse. Soon it was obvious that esthetic concerns about window treatments and the like were the least of the problems with this project. Work had come to a halt before the siding had even been put on the walls.

The young man who started this project went bankrupt. It was a mess.

But in those days, I was at a high point with my business. I had successfully completed several important projects that had made a positive impact on downtown. Both the city government and DARE, by then being run by Susi Hamilton, asked me to come to the rescue.

It seemed like a thankless task, but then I've never been all that concerned about thanks. It looked like something I could tackle. And so I did.

Recently a friend reminded me of something that happened in 2003, right after I had agreed to take this on. During a city-sponsored boat tour on the Cape Fear River, our vessel passed the foot of Nun Street, where Governor's Landing was sitting derelict, its unpainted plywood sheathing already turning gray from a couple of years of sun and rain. Someone asked me about it. Maybe with a bit too much confidence, I replied, "We'll put lipstick on that pig."

An injection of needed capital, some expertise from having completed other residential projects, and a bit of determination were enough to get it done. When the completed condos went on the market, they quickly sold, and they are now among the Historic District's most valuable properties. In 2025, these townhomes, each a bit less than 3,000 square feet, are valued at nearly $1 million each.

The work included extending the Riverwalk past Nun Street. The city didn't want to do this. I needed an access to the project's boat docks, so I built the Riverwalk extension in front of my project. Once it was done, I donated it to the City of Wilmington. And now, twenty years later, our waterfront promenade's southern end is still right there, in front of Governor's Landing. Maybe someday it will get extended the remaining quarter of a mile to the city's boat ramp at the end of Castle Street. But for now, I'm happy that the Riverwalk that started with DARE's help in 1981 now runs a full two miles from Nun Street on the south to the Northeast Cape Fear River Bridge on the north, encompassing all of downtown Wilmington.

It's one of the best projects I've ever done. I'm very proud of Governor's Landing.

Saving Our Hospital

I wish I had more positive to say about this particular cause.

I'm sorry to say that, despite an alliance with plenty of influential people, we were unable to stop the New Hanover County Commissioners' decision in 2020 to sell off our public hospital to the highest bidder.

New Hanover Regional Medical Center, as it was known in its final decades as a public institution, had opened in 1967. It was the result of consolidating the formerly segregated James Walker Memorial Hospital and the all-Black Community Hospital.

Over the next half century, a long series of additions and expansions helped NHRMC keep up with advances in medicine and build an enviable reputation for quality care. I had the honor of being a member of the hospital's Board of Trustees in the early 1980s. When the sale went through, it had 700 beds and was also a major employer, providing around 7,000 jobs.

* * *

In July 2018, by a three-to-two vote, the County Commissioners adopted a "resolution of intent" to sell the county-owned hospital. They had to sell it to save it, the hospital's leadership was arguing. Changes in the health-insurance industry, as well as government regulations, they asserted, were threatening the hospital's cash flow. Without the backing of a large corporate owner, it might not be able to keep up with economic change, the argument went.

Not everybody bought this. Many savvy, knowledgeable people, some with deep experience in corporate finance, insurance, and other relevant fields, disputed the hospital leadership's assertions. Even North Carolina's state Treasurer Dale Folwell weighed in against the idea.

Those of us who wanted to keep our hospital under local control organized under the "Save Our Hospital" name. We tried to rally public support. We held news conferences. We did interviews with any local media that showed an interest in the matter.

In December 2019, I was interviewed for *Encore*, a now-defunct weekly that specialized in the arts and entertainment. "We believe NHRMC, a financially viable institution," the paper quoted me, "is fully capable of managing its own future without selling out or obtaining a partner. We favor local control of our hospital system. And we are confident a large number of people in New Hanover County and Southeastern North Carolina feel the same."

But the hospital's board of trustees and top managers, a majority of the County Commissioners, and would-be buyers had their own case to make. Selling the hospital, they promised the public, would let a deep-pocketed corporation make major investments in our local health-care infrastructure. Novant, ultimately the successful bidder, promised to invest over $3 billion in our region if it got control of NHRMC.

We were never able to break through the arguments of the hospital sale's proponents. Among their most influential tactics was to dangle a bright, shiny object in front of the public and the decision-makers: The prospect of a huge financial windfall to New Hanover County. Just think what we can do with a billion dollars! Clinching the sale was the promise that this money would go into the newly created non-profit New Hanover Community Endowment, which would parcel out a portion of the sale proceeds to community causes every year.

Of course, the money this endowment got wasn't so much a windfall as it was a partial return on the huge public investments into the hospital over its history. But ultimately, that dazzling sum, $1.25 billion, was enough to seal the deal. On Oct. 6, 2020, the County Commissioners voted four to one, with only Commissioner Rob Zapple saying "no," to approve the sale. Even as this was happening in the Old Courthouse, protesters outside on

Princess Street were waving signs; passing motorists were honking their horns. A news report at the time noted that the $1.25 billion sale was one of the largest transfers of wealth North Carolina had ever seen.

In retrospect, many of the perils our "anti" group warned about have materialized. Novant has struggled to keep many of its promises. Under its management, our hospital's performance has lagged in many metrics. Employees were laid off and morale suffered among those who remained. Promises of new investments have been hard to evaluate, since the hospital's financial accounts are now proprietary secrets. The endowment set up to disburse the sale proceeds has gone through its own turmoil, which included the firing of its first chief executive and the resignation of a successor.

This is a hugely complicated matter, of course. But the fact is, Save Our Hospital failed to make our case with New Hanover County's key decision-makers. We weren't able to get the critical mass of public support that other coalitions, working on other controversies, had been able to recruit in earlier years.

Sadly, this is an example of how the decline of local news media, especially the loss of a well-staffed, aggressive newspaper, has made it so much more difficult to mobilize public opinion about important issues. At the time the proposed hospital sale should have been dominating the news, the now renamed *StarNews* had shrunk, with scarcely a third of the staff—or the circulation—it had enjoyed in its heyday in the 1990s. The paper's new owners were systematically dismantling its opinion pages, first ending endorsements in local elections, before eventually eliminating local editorials entirely and firing its editorial page editor. That's not to mention doing away with letters to the editor and local op-ed columns, which had long been a vital voice for the public.

So nobody was left to ask the tough, impertinent questions of the powers that be. Nobody was left to challenge the hospital management's fiscal projections, or seek out knowledgeable opposing viewpoints. And even if any of these reporting assignments had measured up to the standards of a quarter century earlier, the paper's shrunken audience meant we no longer had an effective way of reaching a majority of the community's citizens.

In short: If the "Save our Hospital" crowd had enjoyed the kind of media backing we'd gotten on the coal pile or Interstate 40, I think it would have made a difference in the outcome.

Reviving Passenger Rail Service

For more than a century, Wilmington was a railroad town. When the 161-mile Wilmington and Weldon Railroad was completed in 1840, it was the world's longest. During the Nineteenth and early Twentieth Centuries, other railroads were built, radiating from here like spokes from a hub. When most of them were consolidated into the Atlantic Coast Line in 1900, that new corporation kept its headquarters in Wilmington.

When I was a boy, the Coast Line was the city's biggest employer. Its offices, station, tracks, roundhouse, and warehouses dominated downtown's north end. But in 1955, the ACL stunned Wilmington with the announcement that it would be moving its headquarters to Jacksonville, Florida.

Wilmington, the railroad's executives explained, was no longer at the center of the railroad's network. It wasn't even on the main line; since 1892, long-distance north-south trains had followed a "cut-off" track through Fayetteville, ninety miles inland. But even as the city braced for the loss of tax revenue and hundreds of jobs, we could at least still travel on one of the passenger trains that originated in downtown's Union Station. As late as my time at New Hanover High School, it was still common for students and other fans to ride the train to out-of-town sporting events!

But that wouldn't last, either. Like every railroad, the ACL was facing declining ridership and growing losses; more and more, Americans were traveling by car or by air. And more and more, the railroads were scaling back service and looking for ways to get out of the passenger train business. The ACL closed Wilmington's Union Station, shifting its dwindling passenger service to a squat little building nearby. In 1967, after a merger with its main competitor, the railroad got a new name, Seaboard Coast Line. The final shoe dropped in 1968. That's when the newly merged SCL ran its last passenger train out of Wilmington.

It was just three years later when virtually every other railroad company gave up its passenger business. Those trains were taken over by the new federal rail service, Amtrak. But it was too late for Wilmington. In its first decades, Amtrak had its hands full just managing the thin network of routes it had inherited. It was able to serve some cities only because state governments offered subsidies.

But even though North Carolina's Department of Transportation eventually would do this, sponsoring trains that run from Charlotte through Greensboro and Durham to Raleigh and on to points north, it hasn't yet

Amtrak's 'Carolinian' train, partly supported by the North Carolina Department of Transportation, passes through downtown Raleigh. A new passenger train to connect Wilmington with Raleigh was the subject of a recent state feasibility study.

been able to extend routes to either end of the state. Neither Asheville to the west nor Wilmington to the east is served by the state-backed *Carolinian* or *Piedmont* trains.

And while a few forward-thinking politicians and bureaucrats held out hope that our rail service might eventually be restored, those dreams got a brutal awakening in the 1980s.

By then, another round of mergers had folded the SCL Railroad into what's now called CSX. That consolidated company was systematically abandoning lines that weren't generating enough freight revenue. First to go had been the route that linked Wilmington to Fayetteville. Those tracks were torn up in 1971. Next was the line that ran westward to Florence, South Carolina, gone in 1977. Then, in 1985, the coastal route through Jacksonville to New Bern was closed down. A year later, our best prospect for renewed passenger service—the original Wilmington and Weldon route, running due north—was put on the chopping block.

Despite pleas to keep the tracks intact, in hopes that passenger trains could run on them again someday, CSX abandoned twenty-seven miles of that line through Pender County. Fortunately, rather than turning the real estate over to adjacent land owners, as it had done with its other abandonments, this time CSX offered that right of way to the state. And so, despite the tracks having been gone for four decades now, at least the route is state-owned and remains available. The same is true for the urban corridor that once carried—and hopefully will again—passenger trains into downtown Wilmington.

If you're new to Wilmington, you may not know why there's a sunken, grassy strip through downtown, bridged by North Third, Fourth, Fifth, and Sixth Streets. That's the right of way where the tracks once ran.

Fast-forward to 2023. North Carolina's portion of the Amtrak network was doing significant business, with ridership on the *Piedmont* and *Carolinian* setting records and growing steadily. Amtrak had, after a fashion, linked Wilmington to its station at Wilson via the so-called "Thruway" bus service, which also serves Jacksonville, Kinston, and Goldsboro. It isn't a train, but it is something. Meanwhile, a billion-dollar Amtrak investment to buy and rebuild the tracks on another abandoned right of way in North Carolina and Virginia, the so-called "S Line," promised to cut significant time and distance off travel from Raleigh to Richmond—as well as to the main line north to Washington and New York. And increasingly, state transportation officials were considering establishing new routes, with serious discussion of service to both Asheville and Wilmington.

That was encouraging talk. But actually getting those new routes would take a major effort. So in collaboration with Steve Unger, a Pender County journalist and civic activist, I formed Eastern Carolina Rail, Inc., and created a website, *easterncarolinarail.com*. Our stated purpose was to "undertake a public support drive and do whatever is necessary to assist the NCDOT in making this project a reality." As with so many other causes over the years, we believed that a joint private and public undertaking would work best to create awareness and solve problems.

At the same time, with infrastructure grants from the Federal Railroad Administration, the state finally began serious study of seven new potential rail corridors. One of them runs from Raleigh through Selma and Goldsboro to Wilmington. The $500,000 grant for our route covers what the state's rail experts call "scoping." That work is supposed to be complete in 2025.

Already, it has produced a feasibility study. That projects the entire new Raleigh-to-Wilmington route could be serving 310,000 riders a year by 2045, with 125,000 of them going to or from Wilmington itself. That estimate was based on three round trips a day, with a travel time of two hours and thirty-five minutes each way. Capital costs, including rebuilding and upgrading track and bridges, building or renovating stations, and buying rolling stock, would be $810 million. Once running, though, net operating and maintenance costs would be just $12 to $14 million a year.

That study makes a point of mentioning our Eastern Carolina Rail organization as an indicator of the Wilmington area's interest in passenger rail service.

Further development, including detailed planning, will depend on future federal grants and state matching funds. At this writing, any new federal grants for Amtrak appear in jeopardy from an administration that detests passenger trains. Even so, I am trying to be optimistic that sanity will return to Washington. Ideally, Eastern Carolina Rail, Inc., can help let decision-makers there and in Raleigh know that Wilmington wants to see passenger trains again.

The FRA says it typically takes seven to twelve years from the time planning starts until the first trains run. So if this process isn't interrupted—a big "if"—we might see Amtrak trains here sometime between 2028 and 2035. Because tracks and a major bridge would have to be rebuilt on twenty-seven miles of our right of way, the longer timeline seems more realistic.

I may not be around to see that first passenger train roll into town, but with any luck the next generation will benefit from my work.

Landmark Status for New Hanover High School

When I graduated from New Hanover High School in 1962, the elegant brick building on Market Street was forty years old. At the time, when public schools in North Carolina were still segregated, it was one of two high schools in New Hanover County. It accommodated only White students. Just six blocks away, the county's Black students attended Williston High School.

That would change in 1968, a full fourteen years after *Brown v. Board of Education* had outlawed racial segregation in education. Our Board of Education finally desegregated New Hanover County's schools. While Williston's many devoted alumni and community supporters mourned its closing—it became a junior high school, and is now a middle school—there was some logic to the school board's difficult decision: A racially integrated school system didn't need two high schools so close to each other.

So starting in 1968, New Hanover High School, along with the newly built Hoggard High School, would serve students of all races. As our population grew, two more conventional high schools would be built: First Laney, in the county's northern area, then Ashley, to the south, toward Carolina Beach. (We also now have two small "early college" high schools,

New Hanover High School opened for classes in 1922. The building's future is in doubt.

one linked with Cape Fear Community College and the other with UNC-Wilmington.)

I offer this quick history to give some context to why the original New Hanover High School building, now 103 years old, is so significant. It is the last of its generation of large urban high schools to survive in this corner of North Carolina. It remains an imposing presence, as anyone who drives down Market Street between Thirteenth and Fifteenth Streets knows. Its architecture is distinctive and noteworthy, and it's a major contributor to the city's historical fabric.

The 1922 building was designed in the Beaux Arts style, which developed in the late Nineteenth Century. That's very rare in Wilmington. It was the work of William J. Wilkins, an architect who divided his time between Wilmington and Florence, S.C. (He also designed the Brooks Grocery building on Water Street, which I renovated in the 1990s, and is mentioned earlier in this chapter.) Construction began in 1919, right after World War I ended, and it opened in 1922.

New Hanover replaced the former Wilmington High School, which was North Carolina's first public high school when it opened in 1901. That institution occupied the building on Ann Street better known today as Tileston School—which is now part of St. Mary Catholic School.

When my alma mater passed its century mark, it occurred to me that it deserved some special recognition, and protection. After all, during my many years working in downtown Wilmington, I had seen plenty of other historic buildings either destroyed or so badly altered that they lost their original beauty and charm. That idea gained urgency in 2024 when a member of our Board of County Commissioners floated the idea of demolishing the school rather than investing in necessary renovations. I wanted to head off any possibility that this could happen to NHHS.

My first step was to prepare an application to grant historic landmark status to the school. This was submitted to Wilmington's Historic Preservation Commission. I'm pleased to say that on Feb. 13, 2025, that board voted unanimously to endorse the idea. It also agreed to include Brogden Hall in the application, even though that gymnasium structure is only a youthful seventy-one years old.

Before the commission's vote, I spoke with the *Port City Daily*. "Let's just look at the definition of 'landmark,'" their story quoted me. "It's the feature of a landscape or of a town, something that can be recognized from a distance. I'd say New Hanover High fits that description."

The Historic Preservation Commission's decision put the building on a study list, the next step in a lengthy process. That will take it through the State Historic Preservation Office, which will submit it to a historic review commission. If that board endorses the application, it will go on to the National Park Service. If it passes that final federal review, the high school will be listed on the National Register of Historic Places.

Meanwhile, the school system is proceeding with significant restoration work, which will cost more than $6 million. That mostly affects the façade, where foundation repairs are needed to correct some cracks in the century-old brick walls. Overall, school administrators have confirmed, the building is structurally sound,

They have also publicly worried, though, about how well it will hold up for another thirty or forty years. The County Commissioners have appropriated $300,000 for a feasibility study to answer that question. One estimate says another $90 million might be needed to fully rehabilitate the building. The potential cost of future rehab work, of course, is a possible factor in the landmark designation.

Even if that is granted, New Hanover County, as the building's owner, would have to agree to it being added to the National Register.

As a point of comparison, Wilmington has quite a few other sites on the National Register. They include our Historic Districts, several of which are adjacent to the NHHS campus, and such landmarks as Wilmington National Cemetery and the Battleship North Carolina.

Among the landmark buildings listed are City Hall and Thalian Hall, from 1858; the Federal Courthouse on Water Street, from 1916; and the former nurses' dormitory of James Walker Memorial Hospital on Red Cross Street, from 1921.

While the review process goes on, I'll be watching closely. I'll also continue lobbying both the school board and the County Commissioners to make the necessary investments to keep New Hanover High School a viable place for future generations of students to learn. And as with the other causes I have promoted over the years, I will keep looking for allies who can help in achieving goals that benefit the entire community.

6. What Makes a Citizen Warrior?

As I have thought about what a Citizen Warrior is, I have tried to make a list of the traits that make for effective community leadership.

Here are those attributes as I've experienced them, and observed them in others:

- Firm and unwavering commitment to promoting the health and welfare of your community—of all the people.
- Patience. Don't get ahead of yourself.
- Commitment to success. Be unwilling to accept failure unless all options have been exhausted. Hold on to hope and never give up.
- Effective verbal and non-verbal communication skills.
- Effective personal relationships. These can make you—or break you. You will always need help to achieve your goals.
- Preparation. Do your homework. Pay attention to details.
- Creativity and imagination. With enough thought and deliberation, you will usually find a way to meet your goals.
- Willingness to compromise. You can't always get everything you want. Partial success is usually better than none.
- Follow-through and effective time management. It's critical to stay on top of things.
- Gratitude. Express your appreciation, both to those who help you and to the community at large. Sincere thanks can go a long way.
- Independence. Do not let others control or manipulate you.

- Respect for others. Disagree respectfully but don't be afraid to tell the truth about others' failure to act responsibly or effectively.
- Careful record-keeping. Maintain accurate records of fundraising and expenses. If you form a non-profit agency, it is essential to run a clean operation. Be willing to share your information with the public.
- A stated purpose. Make certain your organization or committee—or yourself individually—is straightforward and honest. Use simple language in stating your purpose.
- A sense of humor. Remain ready to laugh, including at yourself. It can get rough out there in the "court of public opinion."
- Kindness to yourself. Don't be too hard on yourself. You could do better; you could do worse. Celebrate your wins, analyze your losses, and learn from them. (Ask: How can I avoid this circumstance? Or how can I do better?)
- Persistence. Stay at it. Be both persistent and consistent. Always keep your goal at the top of your thoughts.

* * *

Through all my struggles, successes and failures over the years, I've developed a personal philosophy that might be summed up like this: Change is the ultimate opportunity.

Here are a few pieces of free advice for anybody:
- Never stop looking for opportunities to make changes in your life that will benefit your physical and mental well-being.
- There is always room for improvement. There are always better ways of thinking and doing things.
- Improving what you think and do will help you be a happier person, living a more fulfilled life. Never assume the status quo is the best option.

I'm not necessarily talking about big changes, although many of us do face them in our lives. I'm mainly talking about "tweaking," making small, incremental changes.

Are you "tweaking" your life?

* * *

In recent years, I have given a lot of thought to my family legacy, to wondering just what it was that made my father so driven about giving back to his community. I can easily see how his example influenced me and my brothers. But it's not so easy to discern the roots of his motivations.

Here's what I know. Eugene Worth Merritt was a Duplin County farm boy, born and raised near the little towns of Magnolia and Rose Hill. He was a sharp enough student and an accomplished enough athlete in high school that he earned a scholarship to N.C. State University. But that was in the depths of the Great Depression. However strong his personal ambitions were, he felt an even stronger obligation to his family.

And so this dutiful son relinquished his chance at higher education so he could stay home and help on the family farm.

One part of my father's high school education made a strong impression on him—and on me. He was on the Warsaw High School's debate team, which taught him the importance of understanding both sides of an issue. He and the other debaters had to be prepared to argue either position, whether they agreed with it or not. I learned a lot about organizing by switching sides during my own experience in school debating.

World War II brought my father to Wilmington. He was one of the thousands of country boys and girls drawn to jobs at the shipyard here, building Liberty Ships for the war effort.

The family's circumstances improved enough that my uncle DeWitt, my father's younger brother, was able to earn a degree at the U.S. Merchant Marine Academy. Instead of pursuing a career at sea, however, Dewitt turned out to be a hard-headed businessman. Later on, the two brothers would build a successful business here in Wilmington. For many years, the Merritt-Holland company was our region's leading supplier of compressed gases, used for welding and many other industrial processes. (When I was fresh out of college, I worked in the family business for a time, myself.)

* * *

Recently, I have discussed this question at length with my brother John. He has speculated that our father's humble upbringing inspired a drive for "self-esteem" in all of us. The way John explained it was that we needed to find something to make us feel good about ourselves—since we couldn't claim to be the richest, or the most popular, or the prettiest people in town. Instead, as he put it, each of us needed to feel comfortable about that person we see in the mirror every day.

To John's way of thinking, an urge to service may be as much about "a desire to do better" than our peers than about purely altruistic motives.

He has wondered aloud about whether those of us who try to serve are motivated by "an obligation to the community or an obligation to yourself."

And, being honest with himself, he has also speculated that an inherent stubbornness and egotism might be involved, too: "It's as much our arrogance, that we think we know better than anybody else," he said recently. But that also helped us "develop a lack of fear."

When I was pondering taking on the liquor-by-the-drink campaign in the late 1970s, John recalled, "Everyone told Gene he shouldn't do it." It would hurt me professionally, people warned me. Anti-alcohol crusaders would blame me for every drunk-driving accident. But as John saw it, anyway, embracing that cause in spite of the risks was something deep in my nature. He saw how much hostility a campaign like ours could generate, but that I didn't let it stop me. "This is who my brother is," John told a friend. "This is what he does."

But that still leaves unanswered the deeper psychological question: "Why?"

To address that, we have both looked back at how we were raised.

One vignette from my teenage years sheds some light on my father's focus on service. He lent his professional talents and even some brute force to the task of bringing the battleship *U.S.S. North Carolina* to Wilmington in 1962. After being towed to the mouth of the Cape Fear River, the ship had to be temporarily anchored overnight before it could be eased the last few miles upstream. But without power, the battleship had no way to raise its anchors the next morning. So a pair of experts volunteered their skills and their acetylene cutting torches. Alongside his brother DeWitt, my father dangled over the side of the cold, dark, deserted vessel on bosun's chairs, cutting through the anchor chains, so our future World War II memorial could make its final trip up the Cape Fear River. (The chains were attached to buoys, so the anchors could be retrieved later and replaced on board the battleship.)

Eugene W. Merritt Senior's ethical standards were strongly shaped by his service as a Rotarian.

Another vital insight into my father's character comes from his many years as a member of the Wilmington Rotary Club. He joined in January 1952 and remained a member until he died in 1999. True to Rotary's motto of "Service Above Self," he served that important charitable civic organization as president in 1972-73. Then, in 1976-77, he was district governor for all the Rotary Clubs of southeastern North Carolina. (I was a member of that club myself, before and during my time with DARE. As a Rotarian, I took the lead in starting the River-to-the-Sea Run, a fund-raising road race that originally was called the Rotary Run. And now my son Worth—Eugene W. Merritt III—is a third-generation member of that club.)

One of the club's traditions is to send its president-elect to the Rotary International Convention. For my father, that was in June 1972, in New Orleans. Reporting to the club afterward, he commented that rubbing elbows with Rotarians from 151 nations scattered around the globe had made him realize he was "a citizen of the world."

In November 1976, as district governor, he told his fellow Rotarians, "The business of Rotary is the business of service. And what is service? Service is the thing you render above what the price is. Service is an act of love." The club newsletter noted that he also said that whether a club provides service "depends on the exertion of each single, individual member."

John believes that the Rotary ethics our father espoused profoundly influenced all of us. We grew up hearing him quoting Rotary's "Four-Way Test," which asks whether what we think, say, or do is true, fair, aimed at good will and friendship, and beneficial to all. When John was in high school, he became president of the Interact Club—Rotary's auxiliary for teenagers—that our father had founded.

On this coin are Rotary International's 'Service Above Self' motto and Four-Way Test of what Rotarians think, say, and do.

What Rotary's culture meant to my brother was to believe we should look for opportunities to help others "without wanting any reward. To make some difference people will remember." What he and I both learned from our father was that service can be its own reward.

Rotary wasn't his only public service. For example, in 1971, he chaired the annual United Fund drive—raising money for what's now known as Cape Fear United Way.

The year after serving as Rotary's district governor, my father filed as a candidate for the state House of Representatives. He ran on a thirteen-point platform. Much of it was general, as in "well-paying jobs" and "full development of tourism." But several points were very specific, including "Four-lane highway and general road development" and "redevelopment and preservation for Wilmington's inner city."

He got elected to a two-year term. When that term ended early in 1981, he wasn't finished. Instead of resting on his laurels, he threw himself all the harder into two important battles, which I've already discussed: Preventing the coal pile from blighting downtown Wilmington and fighting to get Interstate 40 finished.

At the end of 1984, after that year's elections clinched the prospect of I-40 being completed as quickly as possible, the *Morning Star* published an editorial that was highly complimentary: To my father, to me, to John. It concluded by asking the same question I've been asking myself lately: "Why do the Merritts do this kind of thing?"

The editorial writer, my New Hanover High School classmate Charles Riesz, Jr., offered a few possibilities. "Maybe the patriarch of the family is nostalgic for his days as a legislator. Maybe his sons have political ambitions for the future." (We didn't. At least none that ever amounted to anything.) "Maybe the whole kit and caboodle are pigheaded buttinskis with obese egos. And maybe, you cynics, just maybe they care about their town and are willing to put their convictions and reputations out there for all to see. Maybe all of the above."

Where that piece got to the heart of the matter was in its conclusion. It said, notwithstanding what our motives might have been, that what truly mattered was to "have the nerve to *do* something."

Maybe it's really just that simple.

Appendix

About the Author

Gene Merritt is a Wilmington, North Carolina real estate developer, commercial appraiser, and economic development consultant. He is a historic preservationist and an arts enthusiast.

In his career to date, he has been directly and indirectly involved in over 125 construction and redevelopment projects in Wilmington, mainly in the downtown area. These projects have made major contributions to job creation and developing the public tax base.

Over the past fifty years or so, he has been founder or co-founder of eleven non-profit organizations serving the public interest. Most of those organizations are still in operation. A list of those entities is on his website: *genemerritt.com* and also copied below.

Eugene W. Merritt Junior

He served as president of NC I-40, Inc. a public lobbying group that helped secure the funding that completed I-40 from Benson to Wilmington. The results have been an economic and social game changer for southeastern North Carolina and the state of North Carolina as a whole.

He has been awarded a Lifetime Achievement Award from the Wilmington *StarNews* for his work promoting the completion of I-40 to Wilmington, for his work in the redevelopment of downtown Wilmington, and for his work on other important projects in the city. Wilmington Downtown, Inc. and Old Wilmington Riverfront Celebration, Inc. (Riverfest) have also awarded him Lifetime Achievement Awards. In 2025, the Wilmington Rotary Club honored him with its Leaders in Service Legacy Award. Over the years, he has been recognized for his public achievements in both local and state-wide news media coverage and editorials.

He is the author of many magazine and newspaper articles over the years and published the book *Dare to Dream* about the revitalization of downtown Wilmington. This book, *Citizen Warrior,* aims to teach ordinary people how to be community leaders.

He is currently serving as vice-president of Eastern Carolina Rail, Inc. a non-profit organization promoting the reestablishment of passenger and freight rail service from Raleigh to Wilmington, and is promoting Historic Landmark status for New Hanover High School.

The author with other former executive directors of DARE, Inc., or as it is known today, Wilmington Downtown, Inc.: Susi Hamilton, Gene Merritt, Ed Wolverton, Bob Murphrey, John Hinnant, and Mary Gornto.

Gene Merritt's Organizations and Affiliations

- Committee for a Better Way (promoting liquor by the drink): founder
- Downtown Area Revitalization Effort, Inc.: founding board member and executive director
- Eastern Carolina Rail, Inc.: co-founder
- International Downtown Development Association, Inc.: speaker and consultant
- Leland Economic Development Committee: founder and board member
- Leland Middle School: English teacher
- Mayor's Task Force on City Core Revitalization: member
- Merritt-Holland Gas Company: general manager
- NC I-40, Inc.: co-founder and president
- North Carolina Association of Arts Councils, Inc.: co-founder
- North Carolina Department of Cultural Resources: director of public relations
- North Carolina Downtown Development Association, Inc.: co-founder and first president
- North Carolina State Ports Authority: director of advertising and public relations
- Save Our Hospital, Inc.: founder
- United Arts Council of Greensboro, Inc.: executive director
- Whiteville Downtown Development Association, Inc.: executive director
- Wilmington Improvement Committee (opposing downtown coal pile): founder & executive director
- Wilmington Road Runners, Inc.: co-founder

About the Co-author

John Meyer is a writer and editor in Wilmington, North Carolina. He is a native of Ohio, where he got his education and began his career in newspaper journalism.

While working as a reporter and editor for Wilmington's *Morning Star* and *Sunday Star-News*, he wrote about many of the issues and events this book describes, and supervised later coverage of these stories by many

John Meyer

other reporters. As a *Star* reporter from 1976 through 1982, he covered the City of Wilmington, New Hanover County, and state government and politics. A major focus of his work on the city beat was the first years of downtown revitalization. As city editor, 1982-1985, he directed the newspaper's local-news reporting staff and the New York Times Regional Newspaper Group's bureau in Raleigh. From 1985 through 2000, he was managing editor, responsible for all day-to-day operations of the newsroom, and supervising NYTRNG's Washington, D.C. reporter. In 1996, he created the *Morning Star*'s first website.

Since leaving the newspaper, he has been a partner in his family-owned business, Cape Fear Images, which among other ventures published the *Wilmington Today* visitor guidebook and the *Cape Fear Wedding* bridal planning book, as well as designing and managing those publications' parallel websites. His company produced the annual Cape Fear Wedding Show from 2007 through 2013. In November 2010, that show was the first event in the brand-new Wilmington Convention Center—built on what in 1981 had been intended as the site of a coal-exporting terminal.

1979: Governor Jim Hunt presents John Meyer with a writing award from the North Carolina Press Association.

Starting in 2001, he served for eight years on the DARE, Inc. (later Wilmington Downtown, Inc.) Board of Directors, and was its vice-president for marketing.

Since 2003, he has been a member of the Wilmington Rotary Club, serving on its Board of Directors and, in 2015-16, as the club's president.

Most recently, he has worked as a book editor and ghostwriter, helping many novelists and non-fiction authors prepare their books for publication.

In 2023, Cape Fear Images published his own novel, *Silver*, based on his grandfather's experiences in rural Virginia during the Civil War and Reconstruction. He has also collaborated with a niece, Judith Meyer of Long Beach, California, on the fantasy novel *Midnight Justice*, published in 2024 under the pen name "J.J. Meyer."

Index

ABC: *See* Alcoholic Beverage Control
Adams, Allen: 117-120
Adams, Brock: 107
"adult" bookstores: 2, 6, 10-11, 19, 35, 39, 45-47, 58
Alcoholic Beverage Control: 63-64, 69-70, 73-77, 136
Alper, George: 64
Altman, Joan: 140
aluminum smelter: 80
Almont Shipping Co.: 88
American Coal Export Co: 81
Amtrak: 156-157
Anderson, Charles "Andy": 49, 121-122, 129
Apple Annie's Restaurant: 75
archives: *See* Division of Archives and History
Arts Council of the Lower Cape Fear: 33
Asheville, N.C.: 29, 95, 156-157
Ashley High School: 159
Associated Press: 124
Atlantic Coast Line railroad: 7, 8, 32, 33, 80, 82, 90, 127, 155
Augustine, Joe: 59, 74, 84
Azalea Festival, N.C.: 29, 31, 34
Bain, Camilla "Cammy": 65-67, 70
Bank of North Carolina: 39
Barbary Coast: 60
Barnhart, Ray: 108-109, 111
Battleship North Carolina: 31, 59, 161, 166-167
Belk-Beery: 9, 17, 30, 36, 39, 41, 49
Benson, N.C.: 100, 102-105, 114, 169
Best, Buddy: 60
Bettencourt Arts Center: 35, 39
Blockade Runner Hotel: 75
Board of Transportation, N.C.: 103-105, 107, 112, 114, 116, 121, 123
Bogue Banks: 96
Bordeaux, E.A.: 88
Bradshaw, Tom: 98, 197
Brand, Herbert: 11
Broadfoot, William G.: 103
Brooklyn Arts District: 136
Bryan, Rupert: 65
brown-bagging (liquor): 2, 63, 66, 68-71, 75-76, 90
Brunswick County, N.C.: 64, 79, 81
Building inspectors: 27
bumper stickers: 114
Burgaw, N.C.: 105, 114
Burney, John J. Jr.: 70
Caffe Phoenix: 36
Calabash, N.C.: 64
CAMA: *See* Coastal Area Management Act
Camp Lejeune: 10
Cape Fear River: 2, 12, 18-29, 30, 31, 49, 79-82, 84
Cape Fear Community College: 8, 36, 159   *See also* Cape Fear Technical Institute

Cape Fear Hotel Apartments: 36, 51
Cape Fear Images: 172
Cape Fear Memorial Bridge: 101
Cape Fear River: 2, 12, 18, 30-32, 34, 42, 58, 79-82, 136-137, 139, 150, 152
Cape Fear Riverboats: 57
Cape Fear Scene magazine: 29
Cape Fear Technical Institute: 20, 32, 80, 84 *See also* Cape Fear Community College
Capra, Frank Jr.: 146, 149
Captain J.N. Maffit (tour boat): 18, 30
Carol Coal Co.: 81
Carolina Beach, N.C.: 103, 159
Carolina Savings & Loan: 36
Carolinian train: 156
Carter, Jimmy: 107, 108, 110
carriage tours: 57
Chamber of Commerce: 55, 56, 59, 64, 67, 82, 84, 88, 103, 108-109, 111
Chambered Nautilus Restaurant: 36
Chandler's Wharf (shopping center): 12, 17- 19, 30, 32, 39, 40, 46, 48, 137, 145
Charleston, S.C.: 23, 96, 106
Charlotte, N.C.: 70, 127, 156
Charlotte Observer: 124
Cheatham, Sterling: 148-149
Christian Action League: 69, 71
Citizens for Progress: 87
Cleancoal Terminals: 81-82, 84-85, 87, 90, 92
Clifton, Ann Marie: 44
Clifton, Roy: 44

Clinton, N.C.: 99, 105, 114
coal exporting terminal: 3, 56, 79-93, 131, 168
Coast Guard, U.S.: 17
Coast Line Center: 19, 32, 33, 55, 59
Coastal Area Management Act: 137
Coastal Carolina Crossroads: 89
Coastal Resources Commission: 137-142
Cobb, Robert: 32, 51, 53, 86-87, 90
Committee for a Better Way: 65-67, 171
Committee of 100: 126, 127 *See also* Wilmington Business Development
Community Development Block Grant: 21
Community Hospital: 152
Congress: *See* House of Representatives, U.S. and Senate, U.S.
Cooke, Stuart: 144
Cooperative Savings & Loan: 13, 16, 35, 40
Corps of Engineers, U.S. Army: 39, 89
Cotton Exchange, The (shopping center): 9, 10, 12, 14-15, 35-37, 39, 48, 74, 80, 84, 145
CSX Railroad: 7, 32, 80, 85-87, 89, 92-93, 156-157
Cultural Resources: *See* Department of Cultural Resources

INDEX

DARE (Downtown Area Revitalization Effort, Inc.): 9, 13, 15-17, 20-23, 28-33, 36-63, 67-68, 80, 83-84, 86, 88-89, 98, 127, 137, 139-140, 151-152, 171-172 *See also* Wilmington Downtown, Inc.
Dare to Dream: 170
Dawson's Creek: 157
Dees, Dr. John: 113
Democratic Party: 65-66, 98, 129
Department of Cultural Resources, N.C.: 97, 171
Division of Archives and History, N.C.: 89
downtown revitalization: 3, 11-13, 20-21, 28- 31, 35-36, 38-63, 76, 80, 83-84, 92-93, 138-141
Downtown Wilmington Association: 29, 32, 49-50, 53, 89
Duplin County, N.C.: 99, 111, 113, 121, 128-129, 131, 165
Duppstadt, Andrew E.: 126-127
Durham, N.C.: 95, 156
Easley, Mike: 147-148
East, John: 108-109, 110, 113
Eastern Carolina Rail, Inc.: 157-158, 171
Edmisten, Rufus: 124
Edwards, W. Eugene: 69
Efird Building: 57
Eisenhower, Dwight D.: 95
Elijah's restaurant: 18, 137
EUE-Screen Gems Studio: 146
façade renovation: 10, 21, 29-30, 40, 46, 51, 58, 61
Faircloth, D.M. "Lauch": 99, 100

Faircloth Freeway: 99
Faison, N.C.: 99
Fayetteville, N.C.: 15, 156
federal courthouse, 31, 45, 161
Fensel, Pete: 111
Finkelstein, Ann: 53-54
Finkelstein's Jewelry & Pawn: 40, 54
Fish Market Restaurant: 39, 42-44, 51, 137 *See also* Giovannoni, Ray; Hoggard Building; Roy's Riverboat Landing
Florence, S.C.: 156, 159
Forden, Harry: 135
Foy-Roe & Co: 39, 41
Frankoff, Roger: 23-24
Front Street Brewery: 39, 41
Front Street News: 36
Frost, Robert: 125
Garrett, Garland G. Jr.: 111
General Assembly: *See* House of Representatives, N.C. and Senate, N.C.
Giovannoni, Ray: 42, 43, 44 *See also* Fish Market Restaurant
Girardot, Donna: 140
Goldsboro, N.C.: 147
Gornto, Mary: 23-24, 33, 49-51, 56-59, 62, 170
Gottovi, Dan: 65
Gottovi, Karen: 64, 65
Governor's Landing: 150-152
Greenbriar Hotel: 89
Greene, Harold: 61
Greensboro, N.C.: 1, 10, 95, 156, 171
Griffin, Johnny: 146, 149

Hale, John T. "Tommy": 87-88
Haley, Christina: 58
Halloween: 22
Halterman, Ben: 10, 84
Hamilton, Susi: 58, 151, 170
Hamner, Burks: 75
Hanover Center: 7, 30
Harry W. Adams (museum ship): 18
Hefner, William: 98, 106-107
Helms, Jesse: 108-110, 113, 115, 123
Henrietta II (tour boat): 57
Hicks, Glasgow: 36, 39
Hill, Bob: 71
Hilton Hotel: 74, 89
Hilton Yards (CSX Railroad): 87
Hinnant, John: 58, 170
Historic District, Wilmington: 18, 21, 25, 35, 150-151, 161
Historic Wilmington Foundation: 89
Hodgkins, Sara: 97
Hoggard Building: 29, 30, 39, 42
 See also Fish Market Restaurant
Hoggard High School: 159
Holshouser, James: 101
hospital: *See* New Hanover Regional Medical Center
hotels: 56, 58, 63, 66, 72, 74, 79, 82-83
House Bill 1059: 138, 140-142
House of Representatives, North Carolina: 64, 71, 98, 100, 105, 111, 116, 117, 138, 140-142, 168
House of Representatives, United States: 106-108, 111-113
Hunt, James B. Jr.: 89, 98, 100, 105, 107-108, 110-113, 115-119, 121, 123-124, 129, 138, 172
Hussey, Wilbur: 111
IDEA (International Downtown Executives Association): 52, 171
Illick, Charles: 25-27, 36
Illick, Nelda: 25-27, 36
Independence Mall: 9, 17, 28, 30, 32-33, 39, 71, 82
Interstate 40: 2, 53, 71, 95-103, 168-169
Interstate 77: 95
Interstate 85: 95
Interstate 95: 95-96, 102-104, 131
Interstate 140: 112
Interstate Highway System: 95, 100
Intracoastal Waterway: 2, 137
Ironfront Building: 39
J.C. Penney: 9, 30, 39
J.W. Brooks Grocery building: 46, 136-137, 142
Jackson, Rev. Horace: 68, 71-73
Jacksonville, Fl.: 8, 155
Jacksonville, N.C.: 15, 156-157
James Walker Memorial Hospital: 152, 161
Jenkins, Bob: 25-28, 36, 40, 50
Johnston County, N.C.: 113
Jordan, Bob: 116
Kenansville, N.C.: 105
Kenney, Morgan: 36
Kinston, N.C.: 147
Knox, Eddie: 123-124
Laney High School: 159
Lee, Estell: 88

INDEX

Lennon, Alton: 101
Library, New Hanover County: 15, 17, 36, 41, 49, 51
liquor by the drink: 2, 21, 63-77
Livery, The: 28
Long Beach, N.C.: 64, 140
loan fund: 21, 24, 38, 40, 46, 51, 54, 61
MacRae, Hugh II: 9
Magnolia, N.C.: 4, 105, 165
Market Plaza (park): 29, 31, 34, 40, 42, 45, 51, 57, 59
Marshburn, Carl: 57
Martin, James: 124, 126, 129, 130-131
Martin Luther King Center: 70
Martin Luther King Parkway: 112
Mayor's Task Force for City Core Revitalization: 12, 171
McComas, Danny: 146-148
Mecklenburg County, N.C.: 70
MedNorth Health Center: 135
Merritt, DeWitt: 165-166
Merritt, Eugene W. Jr.: *See note**
Merritt, Eugene W. Sr.: 4, 38, 65, 78, 83, 94, 98, 105, 109, 122, 123, 128, 131, 165-168
Merritt, Eugene W. III "Worth": 57, 167
Merritt, John: 51, 98, 106, 107, 109-110, 129, 131, 146-148, 165-166
Merritt, Steve: 98, 107
Merritt-Holland Gas Company: 165, 171
Meyer, John: 171-173

Mixed Beverage Committee: *See Committee for a Better Way*
Moncovich, Ron: 146
Morehead City, N.C.: 84, 96-97, 102-103, 127
Municipal Services District: *See special tax district*
Murphrey, Robert: 33, 58, 59-62, 139-141, 170
Murray, Malcolm: 9, 12
Myrtle Beach, S.C.: 127
NC I-40, Inc.: 113, 119, 128, 169, 171
N.C. Route 50: 99-100, 122
N.C. Route 55: 100, 122
N.C. Route 210: 125
N.C. Route 242: 100
New Bern, N.C.: 97, 102-103, 156
New Hanover Community Endowment: 153-154
New Hanover County, N.C.: 12, 13, 15, 17, 21, 36, 41, 49, 57, 59, 64-65, 69-70, 72-74, 103, 105, 109-110, 117-118, 120, 128, 143, 152-154, 160-161
New Hanover County Schools: 158-161
New Hanover High School: 136, 155, 158-161, 168
New Hanover Regional Medical Center: 152-155
Newport News, Va.: 80, 85-86
Newton, Michael: 75
Newton Grove, N.C.: 99, 122
Nicholson, Jim: 22, 35
Norfolk, Va.: 85-86, 96, 105
Norfolk & Western Railroad: 85

North Carolina Coastal Federation: 140
North Carolina Downtown Development Association: 52, 171
North Carolina State University: 165
North Fourth Street Partnership: 134-136
Northeast Cape Fear River: 80-81, 99, 125
Northwind (Coast Guard vessel): 17
Novant Health: 153-154
O'Neill, Thomas P. "Tip": 107
O'Shields, Claud "Buck": 64
Oak Island, N.C.: 64
oil refinery: 79-80, 90
Old Town Alexandria, Va.: 42-43
One Tree Hill: 146-150
organized crime: 6, 45
parking, on-street: 32, 53
parking decks: 7, 54, 58, 143
Pate, E.A. "Tony": 65-68
Payne, Harry E. Jr.: 116-118, 120-121, 123-124
pedestrian mall: 9, 14-15, 17, 48
Pender County, N.C.: 113, 125, 128
Peterson, Harper: 143, 145
petitions: 64, 85, 90-93
Piedmont Airlines: 96
Piedmont train: 156
Pilot House restaurant: 18-19, 137
Piner, Jerry: 74
Pollution Engineering magazine: 85, 87
Pontiac Place, 28
pornography: *See* "adult" bookstores

Postal Instant Press (PIP Printing): 25, 27-28, 36
posters: 51, 68-69
Powell, W. Douglas: 69
prostitution: 6, 45
PPD, Inc.: 143-144
Pucci, John: 57
Rabon, Tom: 116-117, 120
Raleigh, N.C.: 2, 72, 95-107, 110, 112-114, 117, 120-122, 124-125, 127, 129, 147, 156-158, 170, 172
Ramsey, Liston: 120
Randt, John: 71
Reagan, Ronald: 108-109
Reaves, Joseph: 9, 12
Redevelopment Commission (Wilmington): 7
Reeder, Rick: 89 *See also* Hilton Hotel
referenda: 56, 59, 65, 68-69, 70-73, 90-93
Reid, H. Van: 64, 74
residential property: 24-28, 36, 58
Residents of Old Wilmington: 33, 89
restaurants: 2, 18-19, 22, 30, 34, 36, 38-39, 42-44, 58, 61, 63, 67-69, 71-77, 92, 137-138, 142
Rhodes, Albert F.: 54
Rhodes S. Thomas "Tommy": 116-118
Richmond, Va.: 72, 157
Riesz, Charles Jr.: 118, 129, 168
River Landing: 128
Riverfest: 32, 33, 34, 45, 50-52, 58, 171

Riverfront Park: *See* Market Plaza
Riverwalk, Wilmington: 19, 29, 34, 40, 45, 81, 136-137, 142, 152
Rocky Point, N.C.: 125
Rose, Billy: 98, 106-107, 129
Rose, Charles G. III: 17, 98, 100-101, 104, 106-108, 110, 113, 125, 131
Rose, William N.: 37
Rose Hill, N.C.: 105, 165
Rotary Club: 22, 36, 133, 167-168, 171-172
Rotary Run: 133-134
Rountree, George III: 146-148
Roy's Riverboat Landing restaurant: 44
Sampson County, N.C.: 99, 113, 129
Sandwich Factory restaurant: 44
Save Our Hospital: 153-155, 171
Schwartz, William: 88
Seaboard Airline Railroad, 155
Seaboard Coast Line Railroad, 155-156
Sears, Roebuck & Co.: 7, 9, 30, 65
Sebian, Kay: 65, 67
Selma, N.C.: 157
Senate, North Carolina: 64, 71, 100, 105, 116-117, 138, 141
Senate, United States: 108-111
Shell, William: 27
Shelton, Stella: 71
shopping centers: 7, 9 *See also* Chandler's Wharf, Cotton Exchange, Independence Mall, Hanover Center

shuttle bus: *See* Wilmington Transit Authority
skid row: 10, 47, 60, 76, 142
Small Business Administration, U.S. (SBA): 21
Smith, William G.: 64, 71-72, 74
Smithfield, N.C.: 99-100, 102-104, 122
Southeastern Mental Health Center: 75
Southport, N.C.: 64
special tax district: 23, 33, 37, 58
Spivey, Jerry: 38
Spivey's Corner, N.C.: 100
Sportsman's Club: 70
Springbrook Farms: 57
Stallings, Livingstone: 97
Star-News (newspaper): 5, 18, 23, 27-28, 31, 42, 49-50, 61-62, 65, 70-75, 85-88, 91, 93, 97, 101, 104-105, 114, 117-119, 121-125, 128-129, 142, 144, 147-150, 168, 170-172
State Ports Authority (N.C.): 16, 51, 81, 96-97, 100, 120, 171
Steigerwald, David: 150-151
Strader, Gene: 136, 142
Sunday Star-News: *See* "Star-News"
Sunset Beach, N.C.: 64
Sunset Park: 68, 73
Sutter, Karl: 35
Sutton, John: 144
Tarheel Magazine: 50
Teague, Vernon: 50
Thalian Hall / City Hall: 161
Three Penny Gallery: 75

TIP: *See* Transportation Improvement Plan
Toms Drug Store: 40
Toone, Edwin III: 35
topless bars: 2, 6, 10-11, 19, 45-47, 58, 76
tour boats: 18, 30, 57
Transportation Improvement Plan (N.C.): 101, 105, 111-112
Trask Coliseum: 55
UDAG (Urban Development Action Grant): 21, 29, 40-42, 45, 48, 81, 136
Union Station: 8, 155
United Arts Council, Greensboro, N.C.: 1, 10, 171
urban renewal: 7
Unger, Steve: 157
United States Courthouse: *See* federal courthouse
University of North Carolina Chapel Hill: 4, 10
University of North Carolina Charlotte: 76, 129
University of North Carolina Wilmington: 24, 55, 57, 126-127, 142, 159
U.S. Route 70: 100, 102
U.S. Route 74: 101
U.S. Route 76: 101
U.S. Route 117: 99, 104, 105, 125
U.S. Route 264: 101, 107
U.S. Route 421: 99, 100, 101, 104, 107, 109, 122
U.S. Route 701: 99, 100, 122
U.S.S. North Carolina: *See* Battleship North Carolina
Utah International Corp.: 81
visitor center: 42, 59, 136
Wake County, N.C.: 72
Wallace, N.C.: 105, 114, 122, 125, 128-129
Walsak, Dennis: 35, 39
Warsaw, N.C.: 105, 165
Warwick, Robert: 108-109, 113
Watkins, Billy: 120
Water Street Center: 143-145
waterfront dining: 18-19, 42, 44, 58, 82, 137, 141
welcome center: *See* visitor center
Whiteville Downtown Development Association, Inc.: 171
Willetts, Frederick III "Rick": 13, 15, 16, 84, 90, 127
Williams, Ellen: 64, 88, 104
Williams Terminals Co.: 81
Williston High School / Middle School: 158-159
Wilmington and Weldon Railroad: 155-156
Wilmington Business Development: 126 *See also* Committee of 100
Wilmington City Council: 10-13, 37, 48-49, 56, 59, 65, 83, 85-93, 103, 135, 143, 145, 149,
Wilmington Coal Transfer, Inc.: *See* Cleancoal Terminals
Wilmington Convention Center: 2, 28, 49, 55-56, 59, 79, 82-83, 91
Wilmington Downtown, Inc.: 20, 23, 171-172 *See also* DARE
Wilmington High School / Tileston School: 160

INDEX

Wilmington Improvement Committee: 85, 171
Wilmington *Morning Star*: *See Star-News*
Wilmington National Cemetery: 161
Wilmington, N.C.: *See note**
Wilmington Railroad Museum: 33
Wilmington Regional Association of Realtors: 140
Wilmington Regional Film Commission: 146-147, 149-150
Wilmington Road Runners Club: 133, 171
Wilmington Rotary Club: *See Rotary Club*
Wilmington Shipbuilding Co.: 165
Wilmington *StarNews*: *See Star-News*
Wilmington Transit Authority: 21, 48
Wilson, N.C.: 101
Winston-Salem, N.C.: 95
Wolverton, Ed: 58, 170
World War II: 165
Wright Chemical Co.: 12, 33
Wright, Julius A. "Chip": 112-113
Wright, Thomas Jr.: 12, 17- 19, 30, 32, 41, 46-47, 53, 137
Wright, Thomas (legislator): 138, 141
Wright, Vivian: 64
Wrightsville Beach, N.C.: 75, 134, 137
WWAY-TV3: 71
X-3 (highway project): 105, 107, 112, 120

Yaupon Beach, N.C.: 64
YMCA: 134
Yow, Cicero: 69
Zapple, Rob: 154
zoning, municipal: 6, 47, 82, 86, 90-91

*NOTE: Because references to the author, Eugene W. Merritt Jr., and to Wilmington, N.C. appear on virtually every page, those terms are not indexed.